The Moment

Also by Larry Smith and *SMITH Magazine*

THE MOMENT

WILD, POIGNANT, LIFE-CHANGING
STORIES FROM 125 WRITERS AND ARTISTS
FAMOUS & OBSCURE

edited by
Larry Smith,
SMITH Magazine

HARPER ● PERENNIAL

NEW YORK ● LONDON ● TORONTO ● SYDNEY ● NEW DELHI ● AUCKLAND

HARPER ● PERENNIAL

HarperCollins books may be purchased for educational, business, or sales promotional use. For information please write: Special Markets Department, HarperCollins Publishers, 10 East 53rd Street, New York, NY 10022.

To read more Moments, and to share your own, visit:
www.smithmag.net/themoment

FIRST EDITION

Designed by Michael Correy
Title spread photo by Brian Lucy

Library of Congress Cataloging-in-Publication Data is available upon request.

ISBN 978-0-06-171965-3

12 13 14 15 16   OV/RRD   10 9 8 7 6 5 4 3 2 1

For Lukas

CONTENTS

Introduction

Moment to Moment

The three-pound weights were hidden by my sweatpants as I slipped onto the scale. With my father standing nearby looking stern and my mother hovering next to him in tears, I realized this couldn't continue. I could probably fool my parents for a little while longer, and maybe my friends, but I was too tired to fool myself: I was a teenage boy with an eating disorder. I could not conquer it myself, and there was no way this was going to end well if I didn't cave in to my parents' request to seek help. That moment of clarity while cheating the scale in their South Jersey bedroom may have saved my life—and certainly spared everyone around me a lot more misery. It's a moment that, decades later, is with me more days than not. I credit that starved time in my adolescence for both an emphatic dedication to food as an adult and a special empathy for anyone dealing with body issues. And you'd never know it, but, like so many of the 125 writers and artists in this book, I've never shared that part of my life publicly before.

I launched *SMITH Magazine* in 2006 with a simple premise: Everyone has a story, and everyone should have a place to tell it. Traveling across the country for readings from our Six-Word Memoir book series, I heard one refrain again and again: "I have the most amazing story to tell you." These stories were always longer than six words, and often revolved around a very specific event that had made a very big impact on the teller's life. From those conversations came the inspiration to carve out space on smithmag.net for what we dubbed "The Moment."

As the stories began to pour in, from famous and obscure contributors alike, we heard how the simple question "What was your Moment?" was spurring conversations across dinner tables, on bar stools, beach blankets, and especially in schools. We are particularly delighted to feature Moments that began as assignments in a number of classrooms, including two each from Ramona Pringle's interactive-design class at Ryerson University in Toronto and from Kristen Brookes's writing class at Amherst. The fact that a number of these stories of life-changing Moments—including one from Dave Eggers—involved a teacher amply reminds us of how consequential those relationships can be. That this book features never-before-published writers such as Eddie Comacho, describing the moment he agreed to be adopted, alongside Pulitzer Prize–winning authors like Jennifer Egan, revisiting her teenage self and a decisive turn toward becoming a novelist, likewise reminds us of how true our founding premise was. Everyone does indeed have a story.

These stories hit us where we live. Few of us will ever set foot in a war zone, and yet Aaron Huey's "If I Don't Die Today, I Will Marry Kristin Moore" evokes a Moment for anyone who's been jolted to take action. Jennifer Thompson's "Forgiven," about confronting the man she wrongfully sent to jail, reminds us of our own Moments in which we must find a way to reconcile a wrong and move forward. Author Steve Almond was the lucky recipient of a handwritten fan letter from John Updike, yet most of us have been blessed with praise—from a friend, relative, or mentor—that inspired us to continue on a path, passion, or career. Everyone has a first-kiss Moment, and three authors (along with some short-form storytellers via smithmag.net) shared theirs. We bet you'll see a little bit of yourself in these lip-smacking remembrances—the good, the bad, and the embarrassing.

For these stories of kisses and kindnesses, grade school injustices and intense revelations, unexpected meetings and unforgivable transgressions, disappointments and delights, births and deaths, I thank everyone who has generously shared a life-changing Moment. Like a personal secret that needs to be released, revealing a moment that changed your life—for good, for bad, or even for worse—is an offering: a connection to others that we rarely make in our day-to-day lives.

This book of Moments represents just a fraction of the stories we received. Hundreds more—in words, images, and even tweets—can be found at www.smithmag.net/themoment. Everyone has a Moment, and we hope you'll be moved to share your own.

Larry Smith
Brooklyn

The Moment

Flash

Caroline Paul

Black smoke was pumping heavily from the house when we arrived. The chief looked unhappy; the first arriving crews hadn't pinpointed the fire yet, and the situation was devolving. My crew was trained for search and rescue, and that was all we were supposed to do, but today the chief growled, "Grab a hose and find the goddamn thing." My partner for the shift was Victor. He was a baker in his off time and I liked him immensely, but he had a maddening tendency to do everything slowly and very carefully. So I had to wait behind for him, and, much to my dismay, Frank got to the nozzle first. Frank was a third-generation firefighter; he was aggressive, eager, and strong. Still, *I* wanted to be on the nozzle, the one who faced the fire head-on. Too late. Frank and his partner were charging into the garage, pushing open a side door. I followed, with Victor trailing.

As one of the few females in the San Francisco Fire Department, I had a lot to prove; the men viewed girls as sissies, I thought, and I had been put on God's dear green earth to show everyone otherwise. To that end, I jostled to grab the Jaws of Life before anyone else, gleefully attended the most gruesome amputations, grinned about the biggest, baddest fires. I once jumped across an alley, from one building to another, five stories up, in full fire gear. I did it because another firefighter had done it, and I figured that if he did, I had better too. No one else would do it. They waited for a ladder to be brought up and thrown across, like smart people.

I was young and arrogant and flippant. God, I was a pain in the ass. And, of course, my comeuppance was nigh.

The situation now in the house's hallway was pretty typical—pitch black from smoke, and hot. Very hot. We were all crawling, dragging hose, bumping into walls and each other. Then—it was this simple—the world exploded. Later it would seem fitting that my turning point arrived the way a revelation should: with a great flash of light. The next second we were in the garage, untangling from each other. I sat up, dazed. Someone said, "Flashover!"

Flashovers are no joke. In technical terms, according to Wikipedia, flashovers happen "when the majority of surfaces in a space are heated to the autoignition temperature of the flammable gases, also known as Flash Point. Flashover normally occurs at 500 degrees Celsius (930 degrees Fahrenheit) or 1,100 degrees Fahrenheit for ordinary combustibles, and an incident heat flux at floor level of 1.8 Btu/foot."

Put it in plain English: The air somewhere near us had exploded into flame.

Now there were curses from Andy, and Frank was grabbing each of us by the shoulders and shouting, "Are you okay?! Are you okay?!" We were, it seemed. All this took only a few seconds, then Frank said, "Where's Victor?"

Victor? He wasn't in the garage. Which meant he was still inside. I processed this in what seemed like slow motion. Everything took on a surreal drawn-out quality. Frank, turning back the way we had so unceremoniously come, Andy's curse words like a long, slow yawn in my ears. Victor was my partner, therefore my responsibility. But suddenly I was frozen, stuck to the floor in some strange, paralyzed state I had never felt before.

And here was the thought, loud in my head and spoken in no uncertain terms: *I'm not going back in there.*

It was only a second. But I heard the voice clearly. I squashed it, just as quickly. Then, as if fighting against a greater force in me, I clumsily followed Frank. We found Victor quickly; he was unhurt, thankfully, and had taken cover in an adjoining room. Later at the station, we joked about the explosion, our burned ears, the expression on the chief's face as we came somersaulting out of the doorway into the garage.

But that day, for me, was more than just another adventure. It had exposed something that I had not reached before—a limit. The explosion had shaken something loose—a dark and fearful side I had to face. I had been young and arrogant and flippant.

Now I was just young.

Chalk Face

A. J. Jacobs

My fourth-grade science teacher, Mr. Campbell, was a full-fledged, capital-G Grown-up. How could he not be? He was a teacher, after all. You want further proof? He had a beard. At least he seemed so grown-up at the time. Looking back, he was probably just out of college, maybe twenty-three, his beard wispy and thin.

Mr. Campbell taught us science—geology, climates, eclipses, the usual. Or he tried to teach us anyway. He spent a lot of the time asking us to keep our butts in the seats and refrain from flatulent sound effects. The usual.

One day, we were being particularly rambunctious. But still, I didn't see it coming. It happened right after Steven Fischer shouted his nonsensical catchphrase "schweeee!" for the fourteenth time. Mr. Campbell snapped. He pivoted from the blackboard, where he was writing the characteristics of sedimentary rock, and whipped the chalk right at Steven's head.

As soon as the chalk left his fingers, Mr. Campbell's face changed. He looked confused. He looked scared.

"I'm sorry," he said. "I really shouldn't have done that."

What? This was definitely odd. The teacher was apologizing to *us*. And the chalk hadn't even hit Steven—it had flown past his left shoulder. I'd seen grown-ups scream and shout and lose their temper. But the saying sorry to kids? And the fawn-like fright?

It was the first time it really sank in that grown-ups are not flawless authority figures. They don't know what they're doing a lot of the time (80 percent, in my case). They're scared of consequences, like a lengthy Time Out from their jobs (Mr. Campbell was lucky, because we never reported his flip-out).

I've forgotten what Mr. Campbell taught me about igneous and sedimentary rock formations. But the lesson about adults being screwups? That stays with me. Which is why I believe you should treat grown-ups as you would a fourth-grade kid, with equal parts skepticism and compassion.

> *"He pivoted from the blackboard, where he was writing the characteristics of sedimentary rock, and whipped the chalk right at Steven's head."*

Shot

Dean Karnazes

I blame my life-defining moment on one thing: bad tequila. Actually, there were probably deeper forces at play, but the tequila shots are what induced action.

It was approaching midnight on the eve of my thirtieth birthday, and I was doing what most red-blooded American males do on their thirtieth birthday: I was in a bar getting hammered with my buddies.

There was certainly plenty to celebrate. I was a young professional with a cushy corporate job. Every month I received a fat paycheck. I drove a plush company car and was treated to all the accompanying lavish perks an MBA of my stature expected. By all accounts, I was successful.

But I was miserable. There was no passion in my life, no intensity, no sense of struggle and high achievement. Everything came easy. The things that society promised would bring me happiness left me feeling empty. So I decided, at that very moment, to change it all.

"I'm leaving," I announced to my friends.

"Where are you going?" they asked. "The night is young."

I told them that I was going to run thirty miles that night to celebrate my thirtieth birthday. They laughed, "You're not a runner," they told me. "You're drunk!"

"Yeah, I am, but I'm still going to do it."

With that, I walked out of the bar, stripped to my underwear, and started running south. Running in my silk underwear felt liberating, like peeling away the restrictive trappings of my life. Plus, I didn't own running shorts at the time. Nor did I own running shoes. So I ran in what can best be described as a pair of old gardening shoes.

I hadn't run since I was a kid. Yet running had always brought me so much happiness and self-fulfillment. I wanted that feeling back. So I kept running.

At mile fifteen, I started questioning my logic. The alcohol had begun to wear off and I was starting to hurt. Still, I kept running. And running, and running...

The farther I went and the more it hurt, the better I felt. I ran straight through the night and arrived at my destiny, a town thirty miles from the bar, about the same time the morning sun was rising. I was totally destroyed, completely haggard, absolutely beat to shit. I looked down at my chafed legs and at my blistered feet, and it made me smile. Never had I been so happy.

I didn't go back to work that day. The course of my life had been irrevocably altered. My high school cross-country coach used to tell me, "Don't run with your legs, run with your heart." That night, I finally discovered the meaning of his words. And I had but one person to blame for it all: Jose Cuervo.

The Envelope

Mo Clancy

After years of wondering, I finally had the envelope on my desk. It was a standard yellow manila envelope, the kind in which important documents always arrived. And though I had been waiting for this envelope my entire life, I just didn't have the courage to open it.

I knew the envelope contained my identity, my real identity, the name I had been given on my original birth certificate, which had been sealed on that day. It also contained the name of my birth mother, a death certificate and, finally, a handwritten letter.

There was never a time I can remember that I didn't know I was adopted. My parents felt it was best to tell me early so that I would not be surprised later in life. While well intended, this knowledge actually created a black hole of a question; one that I felt could never be fully answered. Growing up adopted meant constantly searching random faces in crowds wondering if, by any small miracle, one of them was my mother or a brother or an uncle. I was reunited with my biological mother many times in daydreams, with fantasies of her rescuing me from my gray suburban existence and whisking me off to some exotic land. Ultimately, though, I just wanted to look into someone's face and recognize myself there.

At age twenty-two when I broached the subject of searching for my biological mother, my adopted mother went silent on the other end of the phone. "Why? Why now?" she finally asked.

"I just want to know my real mother," I responded, too quickly to catch the reply's nuance.

"Real?" she quipped. "Where was this real mother when you were five and throwing up with a 103 fever?" and she hung up.

I abandoned my search for a while, worrying about the Pandora's box my curiosity could open, not to mention my own fears of being rejected. My friend Anne, who was also an adoptee, had spent years tracking down her biological parents only to have them both deny her request to meet. Neither of them had told their new spouses about Anne, and neither had any desire to bring their pasts into the present. Anne was shattered.

However, at age thirty-three, the black hole remained. My boyfriend's father, to whom I had grown very close, asked me one day if I wanted his help. He knew of my struggle and offered to hire a private detective. It took me a week of sleepless nights and endless pro/con lists to accept. But in the end I believed that I would feel more whole as a person to have a story, or a history, at least.

We hired an adoptive-search private detective, a woman named Pat who specialized in reuniting adoptees with their parents. The only identifying information I had was that my mother had attended Ohio State University and

> "'Real?' she quipped. 'Where was this real mother when you were five and throwing up with a 103 fever?' and she hung up."

had studied social sciences. My adopted mother had revealed this to me after a few glasses of wine and later denied it, but I knew that she had more information than she would ever fully disclose.

By bribing nuns at the adoption agency and researching records from the university, Pat was able to connect the dots, discovering my original birth certificate with my given birth name. My parents were not teen parents: My father had been in law school and my mother was getting her master's in social work. Because of religious differences, my father left my pregnant mother to marry within his faith. My father liked to play guitar; my mother liked to write.

The nuns also gave Pat a handwritten letter that my mother had sent to the adoption agency. And finally, upon further research, Pat discovered that my mother, at age thirty-six, had died in an apartment fire in Dallas.

Sitting at my desk, I flipped the envelope over and over in my hands. Finally, I slid the contents out, first looking at the birth certificate and my given name: Jennifer Lynn Crabtree. My birth mother was Rita Crabtree. Stapled to the birth certificate was a death certificate with Rita's name and an Ohio newspaper with an obituary placed by her family, who, according to the nuns, never knew of my birth.

The last document was a note scrawled on a plain piece of paper. The handwriting was shaky and uneven. It read:

I have been concerned about her for the past three months but have been struggling so with my emotions that I failed to take action to get a response. It is probably part of facing reality as I am deeply confused about my true feelings. Only the future will hold the solace that I made the right decision. Reasoning does little good right now, only faith provides comfort.

Holding these papers in my hand, I realized that we all are where we should be, and that there might be such a thing as fate. I would have been eleven years old and would likely have perished in that burning apartment with my mother.

The envelope contained a life that might have been—a name I would never use, a mother I would never meet. It also contained answers to more than just my identity; it told me of a woman's sacrifice to give her child a better fate. With that, I decided to put the papers away, close the Pandora's box and get on with what was always supposed to be my life.

Love in a Time of Illness

Diane Ackerman

When my husband had a stroke six years ago, I thought it was the end of our long romance. For thirty-five years, we'd been sentimental sweethearts who pledged our love in words. As lifelong authors and word-mavens, we detailed our shallowest and our deepest thoughts in words. Scanty worries and fiery fears drew words. So did rogue fancies. We aired our joys and sorrows in words. We fought, schemed, and ached in words. We played with words, collected words like rare stamps, paved the bumpy road of everyday life with words. We each earned a living, and self-respect, by tinkering with words for enchanted hours. Even on idle days, a faint gust of words always breezed through the house.

Then, the lightning strike. In the cruelest of ironies, Paul's stroke wiped out the key language areas of his brain. Suddenly a lifetime of words vanished; he couldn't speak or read, and he no longer understood anything anyone said to him. All he could utter was one sad syllable: "Mem, mem, mem."

I hadn't a clue how to cope. *Where are the grown-ups,* I thought, *when one really needs one?* It felt like a total eclipse of our world.

Life changed dramatically, and we changed along with it. But that's always the secret to a long marriage, isn't it? It's not really one marriage but several. People change, events change them, and their life as a couple evolves. To stay together and thrive, one has to make space for those changes, including both sun and shadow. We'd always been wonderfully romantic and playful in dozens of ways. The challenge was to keep our long love story alive. Not an easy task, but one that women, as primary caregivers, face every day. It's all part of the adventure of being a life form with a big brain and swervy feelings on a crazy blue planet in space.

As severe as Paul's aphasia was at first, years of formidable work, creative thinking by both of us, and the brain's gift for slowly rewiring itself has allowed him enough language to handle short conversations and even write during his three most fluent hours each day. And despite his left hemisphere stroke (which too often results in severe depression, anger, or both), he seems altogether happier than before, living more in the moment, grateful to be alive. And so our days together still include many frustrations, but once again revolve around much laughter and revelry with words.

He often wakes up too early, finds me and says: "Come and cuddle." Then I'll crawl back into bed, enjoying the special radiant warmth of the already-occupied nest, slipping deep between the womb-like folds of the comforter, and we'll curl tight, linking our breaths. He'll call me his little *scaramouche* (a rascal or scamp), and I'll recall past times together, easy and hard spells, and some of the fun things we've done.

But a brain injury leaves lasting traces that aren't always apparent and can play havoc with one's senses. Some days, Paul is surprisingly fluent, and most days he's logical. Nonetheless, there are times when his mind seems so different that I barely recognize him. And sometimes the illogic really worries me, like when he asked if he could catch the flu by talking on the phone with a sick friend, because "the breath goes in one end and comes out the other."

And yet, and yet, the old spouse I know still inhabits his being. I often see him clearly through the storefront window of his face, his thoughts rapping to come out. I hear him speaking in old familiar ways, crafting a new pet name with Whitmanesque flare, such as "Spy Elf of the Morning Hallelujahs," "My Snowy Tanganyika," or "O Parakeet of the Lissome Star."

And so our duet continues to evolve. Even if we can't go back to that magical land of How-It-Was, we're closer than ever, and designing a good life for ourselves, in spite of everything. As I write at the end of my memoir about our experience: "A bell with a crack in it may not ring as clearly, but it can ring as sweetly."

Subdued by Stroke

Paul West

The truth came about in a most unusual and terrifying way when I went into the bathroom to wash and stared at the face confronting me. As far as I could tell, it was a normal face, perhaps a little pale and thinner than usual. As I stared again, something began to move. Was this an optical illusion sired by long exposure to milk and oxygen? The face moved swiftly in a downward direction, dragging with it the corresponding jaw. The jaw seemed to collapse downward until it seemed to set up a new satellite where it should have been, and the teeth went with it. What I had to do in this circumstance was what all recipients of flummery do, and that was blink. This did not work. Again I blinked and that did not work either. In fact, it seemed to tug my jaw further than before past any line decreed by man or beast. So I kept my eyes open as long as I could, hoping to make the jaw-shifting stop. It did, but leaving me with an inopportune fraction of what my face had been. While attending to my newfound facial hideousness, I notice something else: my right arm fell uselessly by my side and refused all efforts to pick it up. And then, as the full flagrancy of my handicap came to the fore, a big violet rose, shaped like a spider, hung fast to my gut.

The rest is a blur. I felt that each subsequent facial recognition was worsening my appearance. Besides, I couldn't speak to explain anything to my wife. She was confronted with the apology for an elephant man who was worsening in his condition.

Table Time

Laurie David

As dessert ended one ordinary school night, I looked over at my two teenage daughters, then fourteen and sixteen, and was amazed to realize I had actually done one thing right as a parent: insist on a daily family dinner.

When I first started doing family dinners when my kids were toddlers, it was out of desperation, even selfishness. Having little kids wasn't fun for me. My husband worked all the time. I was a new stay-at-home mom, I had no "mom" friends, and two colicky babies. It became painfully obvious to me that there was going to be a long road ahead if I couldn't find a way to grab some joy for myself. I decided to focus on dinnertime—after all, everyone had to eat. This would be the time for cozy moments and sweet memories. I would have focused access to my daughters; just as importantly, they would have access to me. This would be the time for us to "purposely" be a family.

As my kids got older, I was shocked by how little time we actually had with each other. As a mom of teens now, I'm amazed at how difficult it is for family time to take precedence. The ritual of dinner guarantees we have our check-in time together. Dinners provide stability, a safe zone, a sacred place that is regularly more important than watching television, or working on the computer. This ritual even got us through divorce by reminding my kids that even though the family was changing, we were still a family and dinner would be served. Eventually, our kitchen table provided the setting for us all to share meals together again: my ex, and my kids, and now even my new partner and his daughter too.

Everything you worry about as a parent can be improved by regular meals together. The research on the topic is quite staggering and conclusive. But for me the most important reason for maintaining this ritual is that it makes sure we are all connected to each other. In today's crazy, busy, technology-infused world, that is saying a mouthful indeed.

Tattoo

Summer Pierre

The Killer in Me

Michael Paterniti

November in the mountains, and there, on cue, came the snow. We were driving from our boring old suburb in Connecticut, up over the Adirondacks to Potsdam, New York, where my grandparents lived—and where our exotic kin shot deer and trapped wild animals in the woods near the Canadian border. I was maybe twelve, the oldest of four boys, and oh how I loved this boondoggle, all of us pressed together through candy treats and car sickness, temporary wayfarers cut loose in the world. The signs on the highway always rang mystically—Poughkeepsie, Glens Falls, Saratoga—until we veered off at Warrensburg, and started climbing through Saranac, Tupper, and back down through Colton.

Somewhere along our route, a roadblock suddenly appeared. A trooper in storm-gear stepped out of the strobe-lit murk as our wood-paneled station wagon eased to a stop on the icy road, and my father rolled down his window. Serious words were exchanged in low tones. My father nodded gravely, asked a few questions—a habit of his, as if he might crack the case, save the day. Detective Dad. The windshield wipers went *ka-thunk* as the officer's flashlight raked through the car, a beam searching for something other than the awed expressions of four boys in the backseat.

When he nodded for us to pass, we exploded in a chorus, "What's happened?" At first my father seemed to weigh the truth's potential effect on us, then said, "Someone's escaped from the prison at Saranac."

Huh? Then why in the Sam Hill were we pushing on? "There shouldn't be anything to worry about if we don't stop," he said.

After a reflexive check of the gas gauge (enough), after the reassurance of my parents (the over-cheerfulness of my mother seemed to mask a question she didn't ask), after the surge of adrenaline at the image of some runaway killer, fanged and bad-breathed, waiting for us on the road ahead, I shifted my position to the back window, driver's side. Trees blurred in the gray-green dark, and on certain hairpin turns, our decelerations were of such great concern that I barked at my father to speed up. Only one person could get us through this madness—*me!* I was on high alert for what seemed like an eternity, a half hour maybe, until I began to get bored and a little sleepy.

The dark now gripped everything, choking it off. The station wagon slowed again on a hairpin, our headlights scouring a drainage ditch, and crouching there, in a funnel of snow, appeared the figure of—*was it really?*—a man. He was hunched, with hair matted to his head; his nose, a crowbar; skin, a pale purple. Instead of a black-and-white-striped prisoner outfit, he wore a dark jumpsuit. I bolted up in my seat, panting fog on the glass. When I tried to say something aloud, it came out as a lamb's bleat, a garbled half-plea. *Didja see . . . ?*

No one else *had* seen—or heard me—for that matter. And, lo, in that fleeting moment, I realized an amazing thing: I alone possessed a secret knowledge so powerful it might undo the world. My X-ray vision had peered into the invisible, and spied the wild, demonic thing at its center. I was exhilarated both by my fear—we'd passed so close he could have reached out and scratched the car with his claws—and this giddy feeling of omnipotence. Even as we were putting distance on the killer, I wondered what might become of the next hapless family coming up the road? They knew nothing. Only *I* knew. Which left the killer and me in cahoots.

Over the years, I've thought about this moment, about why I didn't speak up, or shout out. I've wondered whether the man I saw was really real, or simply imagined. (And if real, why did I cast him as a killer, rather than, say, a common embezzler or shoplifter?) What was it that I *needed* to believe about that night?

Maybe this: By keeping the killer's secret I instantly ascended from my little life into a much bigger myth. The world—as represented by my teachers, parents, eventually the police—had already begun its age-old cure of youth, scrubbing a boy of his wild ways until one day he might ride the commuter train dressed like everyone else, a prisoner of expectations. But the killer in me longed for the mountain, the snowfall, the hidden furrow in time from which I might spy the oblivious family in the station wagon toodling by, watching until their taillights disappeared around a bend. I kept the killer's secret because I felt both pity and admiration for him. Covered in the matted fur of his frontier expedition, he was, for the moment, absolutely free. By keeping his secret—and joining him there in that ditch—I was too.

To Worry

Amy Sohn

I was twelve the summer I crashed my bike. My dad and I had rented bikes for our family's vacation in Warren, Vermont, and set out in the morning for an hour-long ride, while my mother and younger brother, then seven, stayed at our rental house. There was a problem with the brakes on my bike—they were sticking a lot and causing the bike to wobble violently every time I used them. I got on a steep downhill and was afraid to touch the brakes for fear that the bike would topple from the wobbling and the speed. From behind me, my father yelled, "Touch the brakes!" but I ignored him and flew over the handlebars, ripping my chin open on the blacktop.

I heard his bike clatter to the ground and his feet running up to me. He looked at my face, tore off the bottom of his striped polo shirt and tied it around my head to stop the bleeding. We knocked on the door of a nearby house and the woman drove us to a clinic, where I was stitched up by a nice, bearded Jewish Vermont doctor. My mother met us there and stayed with me in the examining room while my father took care of my brother in the waiting room. The doctor injected a local anesthetic into my chin and said he was trimming the

> **I saw that you could love someone so much it hurt. It made me afraid to be a mother but also deepened my love for her."**

cut so he could stitch it better, just the way you would darn a pair of socks. That was the first time I'd heard the word "darn" used in this way. My mother, who was sitting in a chair behind the table, began to pace the room. I'd never seen her act so strange. "Are you all right?" the doctor said to her.

"I don't think so," she said. "I feel nauseous."

"Let me give you some Dramamine." He left me on the table, only a few of my stitches in, opened a cabinet, and gave her some pills and a cup of water. She took them, and he watched her carefully. He told her to put her head between her legs and take deep breaths.

On the way out, a huge bandage on my chin, I asked what made her sick. I didn't understand. She said she didn't like to see me in pain. I said I wasn't in pain, I couldn't feel anything except the shot. She said it didn't matter, it seemed as if I was. That was the moment I realized that to be a mother was to worry. My mom had never been demonstrative or histrionic, and still isn't to this day. She had always been a cool cucumber, mellow and controlled, and able to laugh through most stressful situations. But after that, I saw that you could love someone so much it hurt. It made me afraid to be a mother but also deepened my love for her. A mother's welfare was linked to her child's, whether she wanted it that way or not.

Near Miss

Kirk Citron

I should have been in India the night of the party. Digging wells, teaching English, making a difference. But there was unrest in the region; just two days earlier, the State Department had canceled our visas. And so instead of winging my way over the North Pole, I was on the Upper West Side of Manhattan. At a bacchanal.

A two-room apartment jammed with young, attractive, horny people. One of my bosses was there. I was trying to impress him. I was also trying to impress a leggy cutie who was wearing—this was the seventies—pink hot pants. Hot pants!

An older woman arrived. (She was twenty-six.) This woman, Katheryn, was on the arm of a thuggish brute who I later found out was her ex-boyfriend.

At some point during the evening I found myself standing next to a piano. Katheryn was there as well. In the low light of the party, I thought she was a blonde. (She's a redhead.) We talked for less than five minutes. Probably about India. Maybe about our mutual friend, the host; I honestly don't remember.

What I do remember is what happened next.

The party wasn't even beginning to wind down, but Katheryn and her ex-boyfriend were leaving. Suddenly she was standing in front of me. She leaned in, confidentially, and pressed a slip of paper into my hand.

"Call me," she said.

Here are all the ways it shouldn't have happened:

I should have been in India.

She was at the party with her ex-boyfriend.

I was chasing another girl.

She was five years older than I was.

Our conversation was forgettable.

I didn't even remember the color of her hair.

But thirty-three years, six houses, and two grown children later, Katheryn and I are still together.

What I learned is this: Life is random.

There's nothing you can do to plan for the coincidences and contingencies that will come your way, and they're likely to be more important than whatever else you think is important at the time. As John Lennon wrote: "Life is what happens to you while you're busy making other plans." Or, in the words of George Lucas, "Trust the force."

Mom's Favorite Movie of All Time

Craig A. Williams

Per my contract, Disney was obligated to fly a guest and me from LAX to JFK, first class. The guest was my girlfriend at the time, a native New Yorker who was horrified by the fact that I chose to give my two additional passes to the premiere to a couple of my closest friends rather than to her family. But this was, after all, my moment. For the first time, after dozens of tries, a movie I had written was being released.

Underdog was unleashed on the North American box office on August 3, 2007. Based on the eponymous animated series, the film was a computer-dog-meets-live-humans update with an all-star cast:

Jason Lee as the voice of Underdog.

Amy Adams as the voice of Polly Purebred.

Peter Dinklage as Simon Barsinister.

Patrick Warburton as Simon's thickheaded muscle, Cad.

Pre–*Girls Gone Wild* Taylor Momsen as Polly's owner, Molly.

And James Belushi.

Had it been ten years earlier, it might have been the cast of a Kevin Smith film. With a talking dog.

There was, as is the fashion in Hollywood, already a script. My writing partner, Joe, and I had eight weeks to completely rewrite that script, which we managed to pull off, and the movie was greenlit. Rewrites are as much a part of filmmaking as craft services, so it was only slightly awkward during the flight when, sitting across the aisle from me, was the guy whose original script we'd rewritten. He couldn't possibly have been nicer. We spent the duration of the flight chatting not about "our" movie, but about maintaining one's sanity in the screenwriting racket and the pleasures of drinking on the company dime. Which often go hand in hand.

A car service picked us up at JFK and took us to the Four Seasons. We had just enough time to clean up and head outside, where a caravan of town cars awaited. The plan was simple: We, the writers, would show up to the red carpet first. It was the only way the reporters and photographers would pay any attention to us. The director, producers, and finally the stars would then make their entrance.

I followed my girlfriend into the back of a town car, while Joe and his wife got into the one in front of us. We pulled away from East 57th Street and headed for the theater in Times Square. I've never lived in Manhattan, but I've spent enough time there to know where Times Square is. Not because I'm a fan of the Olive Garden, but because it's *Times Square*. Who doesn't know where Times Square is?

My driver.

We went in circles, got caught in traffic, me sweating profusely, terrified that I wouldn't be on time to my own movie premiere. I got updates from Joe via text: "Just got interviewed by *Daily News*." "UPI wants to know how dog talks." "Everyone thinks movie is animated."

After thirty minutes, the driver pulled in front of a theater in Times Square . . . where they were preparing the stage production of

Xanadu. I craned my neck out the window into the sticky Manhattan air. Across Broadway, I could see where the premiere actually was. I pointed it out to my driver. "See the awning with the red carpet and all the other limos and photographers? I think *that* might be it." Reluctantly, he agreed to give it a look.

Security waved us through, popped open my door, and I emerged onto the red carpet. Flash bulbs exploded. Reporters waved down flacks for quotations from their clients. In front of me, the dogs that played Underdog and Polly sat quietly, eyes blinking in the flashing light. And behind me was Jason Lee, waiting for his cue to take his walk. With a shrug, I breezed through the chaos anonymously and found my seat in the theater.

The movie itself was a blur. Let's just say rewriting doesn't stop once filming wraps. And I get it: the film isn't on too many all-time great lists—other than my mom's—despite its status as the fifteenth highest grossing dog movie of all time (don't look so smug carrying those slippers known as fourteenth place, *Beethoven's 2nd*). But just after the film ends, there's a moment that directionless drivers couldn't steer me away from and adorable beagles in capes can never steal. It's right there, under the second line of the credits:

Screenplay by Joe Piscatella and Craig A. Williams

A Piece

Melissa Etheridge

've had many different moments where I made a single choice and it profoundly affected the course of my life. In each of those moments, the choice I had to make was between love and fear. Each time that I chose to not crumble or surrender to fear—when I chose love—I was deeply rewarded and doors flew open. When moments appear to me now, it's so clear: Why would I ever choose the fearful path?

One such moment was when I had been diagnosed with breast cancer. Because I was able to take time off work without worrying about my livelihood, I underwent a radical form of chemotherapy. I choose the most intense form of chemo because the doctors said it gave the best chance that the cancer wouldn't come back. I was in chemo hell.

During that time, shortly after the holidays, I got a call from a manager who said that I had been nominated for a Grammy for my song "Breathe"—best rock vocal. I thought, *Oh, the Grammys are in February; I'll be all sick, won't that be interesting. I'll sit home and watch them.* I was thinking, of course, that I would never go near the Grammys in the condition I was in. Then the manager called back and said that the producers announced that they were giving Janis Joplin the lifetime achievement award. They wanted me to perform "Piece of My Heart."

There was the moment, the whole choice laid out in front of me. It was clear. All the fearful thoughts came up: I'm a cancer victim; I'm bald, ashy, and bloated; I'm miserable and frightened. How could I possibly get up in front of anybody and sing anything? And then when I looked at the other side, the loving side, the light side, I saw an opportunity—a door that I could go through. I saw that I could prove to myself that I was alive. That I was okay. That I was going to be okay. That I had the strength to perform. That this breast cancer treatment had not killed me, not knocked me down.

I wanted to stand up there and do what I love to do for a woman that I love, who was a huge influence on me, and sing a song that I had sung for twenty-five years. I was very confident about the song; it would require no work. I would just have to show up and sing it.

Then I had a new thought: *Well, you're going to be bald.*

In my experience with chemotherapy, with cancer, one of the biggest fears that women have is losing their hair. If I chose not to perform, missing an opportunity because I was ashamed that I had lost my hair, what would that say about me and what kind of power would that give to hair, to vanity?

After I hung up the phone with my manager I had some thinking to do. I had to go inside myself and listen to my soul—examine the love and the fear side of it, all the while knowing that this was an opportunity to step back onto the stage. I knew that my spirit, my rock 'n' roll spirit, did not go away and die. I was still who I'd always been, with the talent and energy I'd always had. I just didn't have any hair.

The echoes and the waves of the moment when I called back and said, "Yes, I will perform at the 2005 Grammys. I will sing, 'Piece of My Heart,'" still reverberate with me.

Almost six years later, each week somebody says something about the performance. I've realized that the performance, and the video that lives on and on, has become a source of hope for people. I'm honored to think that my decision to put myself and my cancer out there in front of millions of people came down to one moment—one moment on the phone, a moment of a choice between love and fear, and the decision to choose strength and love.

I knew that my spirit, my rock 'n' roll spirit, did not go away and die. I was still who I'd always been, with the talent and energy I'd always had. I just didn't have any hair."

Unexpected Pleasure

Jonathan Papernick

It had been months since my wife and I had had sex strictly for pleasure. In fact, until we decided to try and get pregnant, we had spent every moment of our sexually active lives avoiding pregnancy, as if a baby were as horrifying an outcome to a night of doing it as a case of genital herpes. But, we were in our mid-thirties now. A biological time bomb had gone off within each of us and we desired more than anything to have a child. But our bodies betray us—and two heartbreaking miscarriages later, my wife wondered if she was broken in a most profound and painful way. Tests showed my sperm suffered from low motility—they were sluggish and lazy as if they preferred to sit around watching television rather than to swim upstream and do the hard work of fertilization. Over the years of singlehood they had been trained too well not to do their job. I worried about whether I was the weak link between us.

It was a warm August afternoon when we visited my wife's OB/GYN, prepared to talk about "other possibilities." Dr. Hardiman swabbed my wife and told us to wait while she took a look at what was going on. I don't remember if I was holding my wife's hand, or whether I was nervous or bored or hungry, but sitting in the antiseptic little office surrounded by clinical posters of the female reproductive system and fetal growth and development charts, I had no idea that our lives together were about to change forever. Dr. Hardiman knocked on the door and told us to come and look at the slide she had prepared under the microscope. "This means you're ovulating," she said. "Right now. Right. Now." It looked like little more than a smear of clear mucus spread out like a translucent palm frond. It was beautiful and strange and amazingly unpretentious, considering the secrets it held. I stared into the microscope at the mystery of creation laid out before me, and could not believe that something as simple as this held the singular key to creating life.

The doctor ordered us to go home immediately and have sex if we wanted to have a baby. And whether we ran out of her office or walked, we did rush home and do what we needed to do, both of us afraid and excited, knowing that if we were ever going to get pregnant, it would be now. As much as I would like to tell my son one day that we did it like a pair of jungle cats so that all the neighbors on our street could hear our bodies in motion, our whispers and moans, I can only say that we did it, and that my slacker sperm did its appointed job.

It is amazing to know that my son, with all his pale-skinned beauty, fierce tempers, anarchic laughter, and baffling idiosyncrasies—a complex universe of wants and desperate needs—was counseled into existence by a savvy doctor who cared, and that if we'd missed that visit to the OB/GYN, or had not taken her blunt advice, or if I had simply misfired, he would never have had the chance of simply being. As my second son proved some twenty months later, surely there could be others, mixed together in a biological cocktail to create the closest thing we'll ever know to a miracle. But, the particular alchemy of that specific day in August was our only chance in a lifetime to create the little blue-eyed boy who cannot sleep without the right dose of snuggles; who conscientiously asks before every meal, "Is there milk in this?"; who knows the word Afghanistan but cannot understand why there should ever be a battlefield; who, for now, still believes his daddy has all the answers in the world. It is humbling to realize how narrow the razor's edge of existence actually is, and how easily my son could have missed the whole show. And how I would never have known what either of us was missing.

Someday

Michael Forster Rothbart

My wife was ready to have a baby. I was not. Sure, I supported the idea in a vague, abstract way—I wanted to have kids just as I wanted to retire to a house on a lake. Someday.

But now? Why now?

Eventually she convinced me by telling me how it wasn't that easy, that many couples try for years before they have kids. If we wanted a baby in a few years, she said, we should start now.

Two weeks later she was pregnant.

Our son was born just after midnight. Some parents—including my wife—say they fell in love with their children the moment they laid eyes on them. I did not.

Here he was: slimy, squalling, wrinkly, cone-headed. Kind of cute, sure, in a Muppet sort of way. But that's not love.

The moment came for me one week later. I was rocking him on my legs, soothing him back to sleep. He stared into my eyes in that

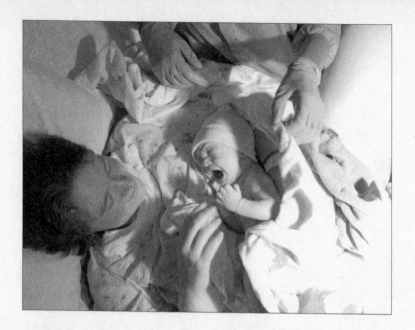

half-focused, newborn way. I let him suckle the tip of my pinkie, and he held on as if he was never, ever letting go. My heart cracked open.

Four years have passed and Jacob is now my closest companion. He should have a sibling. Someday. And my wife has decided that someday is now.

Even an idiot is hard to fool twice. I mull it over, marshal my arguments. Screw up my courage to tell her: Now is just not a good time. The day I'm ready to tell her, she beats me to it: She is pregnant.

No Consolation

Neal Pollack

n the fall of 1987, I traveled to Madison, Wisconsin, to see my grandfather receive an award. Grandpa hadn't been honored much in his life, which had the following arc: A childhood in Madison as the son of a well-regarded judge and rabbi, an undistinguished naval career, ownership of a middling tire store in suburban New Jersey, and a stint as a low-level functionary at a San Diego chemical-supplies company. In the early eighties, he invented a "water broom" that he thought would be his ticket, but someone beat him to the patent. A palpable cloud of bitterness shaded his every action and utterance.

But rather than surrendering, he instead entered a surprising period of collegiate boosterism. Grandpa had always considered his years at the University of Wisconsin his finest. In gratitude, he started raising money for the school's crew team, making sure they got star treatment when they came to San Diego for an annual regatta. My family found this development a bit strange, because the man had never rowed a stroke, but it gave his days shape and meaning. He got to meet all the other rah-rah swells, culminating in one of his life's highlights, a night hanging out in a hotel room with Elroy "Crazylegs" Hirsch, the Pro Football Hall of Famer who was, at that time, UW's athletics director. "He took off his shoes and drank a beer on the bed, just like a regular guy," my grandpa said.

This all culminated in the university recognizing him for meritorious alumni athletic service, or some such thing. He talked about nothing else for months. This was the crowning glory of his existence, and he beamed with hopeful pride. Attention would, at last, be paid. I was already going to be in the Midwest to look at colleges, so my mother and I got invited to bear witness.

He got his award at night, on the stage of the student-center bar. Grandpa beamed as an announcer gave a run-down of all the things he'd done for the crew team. It was a nice moment.

After that, they introduced the evening's *real* honoree, a guy who'd done so much for the university that his accomplishments could barely be listed. They turned off the lights and shone a spotlight.

The room exploded in adulation. Behind this tall, handsome, silver-haired winner in the game of life, my short, bald grandpa shook in the shadows, his false teeth drawn into an even falser grin, his eyes poorly concealing his envy and broken dreams. All his life, handsome go-getters had bested him. This had been his greatest chance. And he'd lost again.

He started drinking more heavily than before. He started coughing. He went into the hospital. On my twenty-third birthday, he called with this advice: "Go to

> "On my twenty-third birthday, he called with this advice: 'Go to Denny's, because they'll give you a free Grand Slam breakfast.' That was the last thing he ever said to me."

Denny's, because they'll give you a free Grand Slam breakfast." That was the last thing he ever said to me. Fewer than six years after his final disappointment, he was dead.

Until that night in Madison, I'd considered life a shining tapestry of limitless possibility. My grades were good. I'd won trophies. The future held nothing but fortune, success, and happiness. But for the first time, in my grandpa's face, I saw the possibility of failure, not just temporary setbacks, but the end of all earthly hopes.

Though I'd hardly characterize my years since then as being defined by unrealized potential and lack of success, I do know what it's like to slump in the background while someone else gets handed the prize. It's a feeling you have all too often as an adult. When my grandpa died, he only left me an old pair of flip-flops and his tattered copy of *Doc Savage: The Man Of Bronze*, but his real inheritance was this: the knowledge that things can, and probably will, eventually go badly in small, sad ways. I suppose I should be thankful, but, somehow, I'm not. I carry that moment like a heavy pack, and I keep waiting for an invitation to put it down.

Checkpoints

Alaa Majeed

During the burning summer of 2004, in the holy city of Najaf (the Shiites' Mecca, south of Baghdad), I was covering a battle between the US Army and the Jaish al-Mahdi, an ideological militia led by Shiite anti-American cleric Muqtada al-Sadr.

Our plan was to get into the Imam Ali shrine to, first, see how the Iraqi locals protesting in defense of the shrine were doing, and second, to collect two Western journalists who had been reporting from the shrine but got stuck inside when the fighting turned heavy. To preserve our safety, we reporters needed to secure a "permission" from the US military to cross the battle line. We also needed a green light from the Jaish al-Mahdi, or JAM (as the US military named them), in case they assumed we were spies or American allies. To prevent a fatal incident, we carefully described ourselves to the JAM, informing them of when we intended to go to the shrine.

I sat in the back of a white Corolla that led the convoy of seventeen other vehicles driving to the shrine. In addition to the large sticker signs on the vehicles, which read "TV" or "media" in both Arabic and English, our driver waved a white flag as he drove. The desolate streets through which we passed looked insidious; I was used to seeing them crowded and full of life. US forces had bombed houses and other buildings to the ground. The city looked like a ghost town.

When we made it to the first US checkpoint, we were stopped and questioned before being advised to turn back. We thanked the American soldiers, but continued. Then we heard warning shots from JAM snipers, who walked toward us, pointing their guns at the car in which I was riding. I was between two female Western journalists who clung to my arms when they heard the shots and saw the pointed guns. Although we had informed the JAM spokesperson of our plans, the snipers seemed quite surprised when we showed up.

From that point on, we continued our trip on foot. We were about a mile away from the shrine. Wires attached to explosives filled the place, but the JAM were nice enough to warn us of how to steer clear of these.

When we finally got to the shrine, a big, weary-looking Iraqi man approached me. He asked me to follow him. He took me to a room that looked like a small clinic. Inside, I saw a man in his thirties lying on a bed. He was bleeding heavily from several places, including his head, and his thighs were missing flesh. Five men stood watching the wounded man and crying. I was devastated as I watched his life fading away. I was told that he had been caught in a battle, but had nothing to do with the fighting, that he was a doctor and spoke seven languages, and that he would only be saved if I could help get him to the hospital. I didn't know what to say, but I went to my team to get a sense of whether we could rescue him. They told me that they wouldn't do it. My driver made a big hullabaloo about it. With tears falling, I went back and said that I couldn't help.

We collected the two journalists and spoke with other Iraqis before heading back to our hotel. Concern about the wounded man led us to return the next day. I saw the same Iraqi who had spoken with me the day before. This time, he looked accusingly at me and said sadly that the wounded man had died. I cried and cried. Did it matter in the least whether that man was a fighter? No. To me, he was a human being, someone who looked like my father when he was younger, or my brother now. I still can't stop thinking that he might be alive if I could have taken him to be treated.

Seven years later, the guilt of being a journalist who is unable to be a human being first follows me, refusing to let me rest. I still can't let that moment go.

The Assignment of My Life

Ruth Gruber

I was born one hundred years ago in Brooklyn's Williamsburg neighborhood, in 1911. I always loved words. In the first grade, I would listen to my beautiful African-American teacher read poetry. She was the only teacher I had in elementary school who was not Irish or Jewish, and her soft voice reading poetry was like music. I was mesmerized. Words—written, spoken, waking me in full sentences from my sleep—became the fuel that drove me. That's when I made up my mind that my life would be about writing.

As a young girl, I was always restless and in a hurry. I went to NYU and finished in three years. My English professor sent my essays to *The Atlantic, Harper's,* and elsewhere. They all got rejected, but with lovely letters. After NYU, in 1931, just as Hitler was rising to power, I went to Germany for a one-year fellowship at the University of Cologne. My professors encouraged me to get a PhD in writing, but how could I do it in one year? The head of the English department, Professor Herbert Schoffler, said, "It's never been done before, but maybe you can do it." I passed my orals, wrote my thesis on a then relatively unknown British writer named Virginia

Woolf—and at twenty years old the *New York Times* called me the youngest PhD in the world.

When I came home, there weren't a lot of jobs in journalism, certainly not for young women. I started sending articles and had enough rejections to cover my bedroom walls. If I had ever taken a course in journalism I would have known that you should "write what you know." Eventually I decided to write an article about what I did know, my home of Brooklyn, and the *New York Times* bought it. That was really the beginning of my life.

I became a special foreign correspondent for the *New York Herald Tribune*. I reported stories from Alaska, the Soviet Arctic, and elsewhere.

I left journalism for a period during World War II to take a job as Special Assistant to the Secretary of the Interior, Harold Ickes. In 1944, he assigned me on a secret mission to be an escort for nearly 1,000 Jewish refugees from Italy to the United States aboard a military ship called the *Henry Gibbins*. I was made a simulated general, so that if I was captured by the Nazis, they wouldn't kill me. That was according to the laws of the Geneva Convention.

I spent two weeks on this hot, crowded ship; we were hunted by Nazi seaplanes and U-boats. I talked to many of the refugees. I told them they needed to tell me their stories of persecution. Many of them said, "How can we tell you? You're a young woman, and what they did to us was so obscene that you just don't want to know about it." And I, in turn, responded that they were witnesses to history, and they had to help America learn the truth about Hitler's atrocities. So they talked and I listened, and I took down, in longhand, everything they told me.

The refugees were brought to and held at a decommissioned military base in Oswego, New York, and decades later, at a 1999 reunion of the refugees in Oswego, several people said, "We know now what happened to many of us former refugees, but we don't know what happened to you." I was 88 at the time of the reunion, and when I looked back at that experience, as well as at more than a half century of journalism, I realized that my involvement with the Oswego refugees was the defining moment of my life.

My time on that ship made me aware that as a journalist I would always be both witness and participant; I learned that I must live a story to write it. And I began to live the Oswego story the moment I climbed aboard the *Henry Gibbins* and met the survivors, many still wearing their striped concentration camp pajamas with newspapers wrapped around their bare feet. Because of them and those we lost, I vowed I would fight with every cell in my body to help rescue Jews in danger. After that experience, I would continue to be a journalist, photographer, and book author. But from that moment on, inextricably, my life would be about rescue and survival.

Photograph courtesy of Ruth Gruber

Make Love, Not War

Jeremy Toback

The night before, I had called my wife, Fabienne, from the dingy green room of the Theater of Living Arts in Philly and asked her for a separation. Then I wept. Very rock 'n' roll.

I was on tour with the band Brad, playing big clubs filled with good people, and getting paid close to enough to cover my bills. On the way up this had been the dream, but it was beginning to feel depressingly like the demise. I didn't believe in the record we were supporting, and I was desperately seeking direction for my solo music during the dull moments between shows. Back in Los Angeles, Fabienne was taking care of our one-and-a-half-year-old son, Miles, catching my calls, which were made from truck stops and lobbies, and listening for signs of hope. Who could blame her for being frustrated and disappointed? Apparently, I could.

I woke early the next morning, October 26, 2002, in front of the 9:30 Club in Washington, DC; that's the fun part of touring, shutting your eyes and waking up someplace else. Stone and I stumbled through the dappled scent of stale pot with little threat of waking anyone, and caught a cab to the National Mall. I threw my voice into the pro-peace chorus, focused my anger on harangues against the threatened invasion of Iraq, and hoped for signs of hope. I saw thousands upon thousands of caffeine-brave faces and cliché banners belying what I already knew: There was nothing we could do to prevent the war. As murderous, illegal, and absurdly costly as it would be, it was going to happen. And, in that moment, I also remembered something my ex-manager, Bill Leopold, liked to say: "Control your controllables." In spite of everything, I smiled slightly; God can be such a deviously ironic dude when she wants to be. So I kicked the wet grass, pulled my cell phone out of my pocket, and called Fabienne. I shouted over the DC protest din and the east coast a.m. fog, "Let's work this out." I guess I achieved some deeper conviction, because she agreed.

There are two genuine miracles that became possible on that crap October day. First, I began to understand that life is a lot more fun when you accept it on its own terms; I still love to fight this notion, and indulge in a little sweet suffering, but I now know that winning is inevitably in the giving up. And the second miracle, the concrete evidence that this cosmic concept yields actual earthly result, is our son, Ezra King, born February 22, 2006, and playing the card game War in the next room, making it sound impossibly beautiful as I type this word, in this moment.

Thank You, Lionel Richie

Matt Dojny

IN **APRIL 2005,** I decided to try and write a novel. I wrote whenever I could find the time: on the weekends, and early in the morning before work, and after work, late at night. ● By April 2008, I'd written about 650 pages (double-spaced) and there was no end in sight. My book had become sprawling and cumbersome and semi-plotless, and I was beginning to secretly suspect that I had no business writing anything at all and that I should quit while I was ahead. One morning around that time, I was sitting on the subway on my way to work, reading a printout of my novel and feeling dispirited and sleepy and slightly hungover. I was having trouble concentrating because the woman next to me was having a sneezing fit, and also because a homeless guy had just gotten on at the far end of the train and was semi-tunelessly singing an unrecognizable song in a weird high-pitched voice and asking for change as he slowly made his way towards my end of the train. I did my best to block him out as I read my story: a secondary character in my book named Mr. Horse had just dressed up as Lionel Richie and was about to get onstage and perform. The homeless guy was getting closer to me now, and I dimly noticed that his voice was actually weirdly beautiful—it was tremulous and halting and pleasingly sorrowful, and reminded me a bit of the jazz singer Little Jimmy Scott. I redoubled my efforts to ignore him, and focused on reading the text— my character had begun to sing a Lionel Richie song, and I'd excerpted some lyrics: "Because I'm easy/I'm easy like Sunday morning/Because I'm easy/I'm easy like Sunday morning." And, as my eyeballs scanned those words printed on the page I held in my hands, a bizarre and remarkable thing happened: at that same exact moment, the homeless guy—who was now directly in front of me—was singing those identical lyrics as I read them silently to myself, as if he were looking over my shoulder and singing my novel aloud to the subway car. He'd been singing "I'm Easy" ever since he'd gotten onto the train, and I just hadn't realized it. The hair stood up on the back of my neck, and I started crying a little bit, and I gave him a five dollar bill, and then he got off the train. ● Soon thereafter, I took a month-long leave of absence from work, which turned into a four-month leave of absence, and eventually I finished the book and sent it to a few literary agents, including a woman whom I'd met at a party and had told this story to. She agreed to represent me. ● My novel is going to be published in **APRIL 2012.**

THANK YOU LIONEL RICHIE

Assembly

Vivian Chum

'm a seventh-grader in a Texas public school on the morning an announcement comes over the school's crackling PA system.

"All seventh-grade minority students, report to the cafeteria." It's an odd request to say the least, but we do as we're told. We are accustomed to following the PA system's commands.

At the cafeteria, the school principal and vice-principals—all white—are waiting for us. There are a few minutes of chaos as African-American, Hispanic, and we Asian-American students seat ourselves at the long cafeteria tables.

"You've been called to this assembly to discuss your performance on the standardized Texas Assessment of Academic Skills test," the school principal explains. And by that, he means our collective *under*-performance on the TAAS test compared to our white counterparts.

Bar graphs projected on a screen compare the TAAS scores of white and us non-white students on the reading, math, and writing portions of the exam.

"Here are the scores grouped by white and minority students. See where the white students are? Here's you. Here is your reading score.

Here is where the white students are. Now let's turn to math."

I scan the cafeteria. Some of the best students in the seventh grade who just so happen to be African-American, Hispanic, and Asian-American are here. I lock eyes with Matt, a half-Asian kid I don't know very well. In his face, I see a reflection of my rage.

By the seventh grade we've all read about racism in history class. That is, we know the word. We know about the Nazis and the KKK. We've done about half a dozen units on the slave trade.

Nonetheless, I don't understand what this assembly is. We aren't exactly being shackled in chains or lynched or even called names. So why do I feel this way?

The lecture drones on. We are reminded that in the not-too-distant future, we will be required to pass the high school TAAS exit exam in order to graduate. We are told that collectively, as minority students, we must work harder, be more focused, and study more. We are reminded that school funding is tied to our performance on the TAAS test. We are again shown a battery of graphs charting scores and passage rates. There's even an analysis by race—African American, Hispanic, and white. Asian-American students are not accounted for.

Maybe it was an oversight that Asian-Americans have been called to this assembly, I think. What's the point in getting worked up about an oversight? But aren't we minorities too? I scan the cafeteria for all the Asian-American kids in my grade. One, two, three, four, five, six if you count Matt. Not even enough Asian-American seventh-graders to form a softball team, much less a majority. Isn't minority the opposite of majority? So are we Asian-Americans minorities or what? I don't know.

What I do know is I want to knock the teeth out of the principal and the vice-principals. I want to spit in their faces, to throw some punches. I want to tear up all the certificates of achievement they've given me throughout the years.

But I'm still. My face is blank. I do nothing.

When the adults have said their piece and we're told we can go back to class now, we shuffle out in silence. By now, I'm numb with anger, and for the rest of the day, I can't stop thinking about the assembly. But no one talks about it, not even during lunch break. It's as if we're embarrassed or would rather pretend the assembly never happened.

Later, I finally mention the assembly to my older and wiser friend Dan Huang (a ninth-grader).

"I would have staged a walk-out," Dan says. I feel the rightness of his words.

I imagine myself standing up in the middle of the assembly, making a huge scene as I pull my chair out from under the cafeteria table. I imagine stepping up on my chair and saying in a loud, defiant voice (one that until now has only made guest appearances before my bedroom mirror): "This is wrong. If you agree, walk out with me now." Why didn't I do that? Why did I just sit there? Why did we all just sit there?

From this day on, I promise myself, no matter what the cost, I will speak up.

The Calling

Baratunde Thurston

I sat on the radiator in the front hallway of my four-dude-occupied apartment in Somerville, Massachusetts, that December day in 2001. My then-girlfriend sat fifteen hundred miles away in her parents' home. She asked what seemed a simple question: "What do you like more: writing or performing?"

At that point I'd done my fair share of both: acting in musicals and plays in high school and college; playing bass in an orchestra for several years as a young child; reporting and writing columns for my college paper; and running a satirical *Onion*-style newsletter called *NewsPhlash*. But now out of school, my life was entirely focused on a different kind of work—strategy consulting (read: corporate Power-Point production). The only evidence of my past hilarity were several e-mails and clips I had forwarded to her.

I answered her question in an "on the one hand . . . on the other hand" style of non-commitment as I struggled to weigh the benefits of live audience energy versus the craft of meticulous word selection within a written piece. Stage allows me to improvise and ride the wave of the room. But I pretty much think with my hands on a keyboard.

After several rounds of this internal debate, she cut me off: "Well, why aren't you doing *either*?"

I was not prepared for this interruption. "What do you mean?" I asked.

"Well, you say you love both, but you're not doing either. Why not?"

Damn. She raised an excellent point. However, I had an excellent response ready. I shared my long-term strategy: pay off these crazy college loans, build up my financial independence, then do my "art" when I could afford to.

She outflanked and destroyed my argument from the east and west.

First, she explained, I might never reach this magical, ill-defined goal of "financial independence" because financial well-being is relative, and I might keep pushing the victory line farther and farther into the future.

Second, suppose I *did* reach the financial goal some years into the future. What would I have to show for the time in between? I wouldn't have written anything since college. I'd be rusty, crusty, out of practice and all around lame. I would have lost "it."

Damn again.

I count that phone call among the greatest speeches I've ever heard. Obama's speech on race during the campaign was pretty good, but The Phone Call inspired me to act. Immediately. I got off the phone and began writing. I resurrected my *NewsPhlash* e-mail list and committed to publishing it every week. Those writings became my first self-published book, *Better Than Crying*.

Within two weeks of The Phone Call I was flipping through the Boston Center for Adult Education catalog and stumbled upon a stand-up comedy class. I enrolled. I applied and got into a comedy-writing workshop going on down in Brooklyn, run by Michael Colton and John Aboud, then of a popular humor website called ModernHumorist.com; every Tuesday I learned something new about the world of comedy from guest lecturers like Andy Borowitz (*Fresh Prince* and BorowitzReport.com), Patrick Borelli (stand-up), Michael Schur (*SNL*, *The Office*, *Parks & Recreation*), and Carol Kolb (*The Onion*).

Sundays, I wrote *NewsPhlash*. Monday nights I got stand-up basics in Boston. Tuesday nights, I raced to Brooklyn for the Modern-Humorist workshop and took a 3:00 a.m. train back to Boston where I got to work at 7:30 a.m. Wednesday, showered and continued making awesome corporate PowerPoint slides.

The then-girlfriend and I are no longer together, but sometimes people leave more than a mark on your life. They can nudge your life in a way that allows you to become who you are supposed to be.

Missed Call

Annie Leahy

I remember the mice—one dead and one alive. I was working from home and I'd just taken a break to make some lunch. I opened the cabinet under the sink to throw something away and was startled by two mice in the bottom of the trash can. We'd been away for a few days and it appeared that while gone these two had found their way in—but not out. One was scurrying around in circles and the other, less fortunate, had already expired. From the looks of it, his friend had been snacking on him.

I pulled the trash can out from under the sink and walked with it into the backyard. At the far end, near the shed, I let the live one out and he took off quickly. The dead one was a bit trickier because he was stuck to the bottom. I walked toward the driveway and grabbed the hose. I pointed the nozzle into the barrel and let the water pressure help release his dried-up little corpse onto the pavement and, floating, into some bushes.

It was September in Maine, and after a depressingly wet spring and a less than impressive summer it was finally sunny and warm. I tilted my head upward, soaking in the sun before climbing the stairs to the porch and walking back inside.

In the kitchen I noticed a light flashing on my phone. Missed call. I was pregnant and had been waiting for a call from the lab technician with our amniocentesis results. When I looked at the number my heart literally broke in two. The missed call was from my doctor. He would have left good news to the lab technician.

I remember just standing there staring at the phone with a deafening silence all around me. You hear stories about people's reactions when faced with imminent bad news—*a police officer at a front door in the early hours of the morning*—just throwing up their hands to make the words stop so that life can remain exactly as it was for just one more moment. I now understood what that felt like. My hands trembling, I dialed the doctors office while at the same time sending an instant message to Mike asking him to come home.

Wicked Start

Gregory Maguire

In the space of a few days in February 1993, BBC 4 went from calling a missing two-year-old boy "lost" to "abducted" to "deceased" to "tortured and murdered." The story was torment incarnate—who could attack a child as beautiful as Jamie Bulger, with a face like a Christmas tree ornament, that toddler chubbiness, that radiant trust? A shocked nation—and I, a lonely expat—soon learned that the villains were two boys playing hooky from grammar school.

British law didn't then require anonymity for a minor accused of a crime, and so the faces of the accused were plastered on every front page and TV screen. Such young lads—the papers said ten years old—and so lost themselves . . . how did they get that way? The chattering classes, as they are called in London, took the subject and ran with it. Dinner party debate, pulpit examination, editorial opinion, conversation in the queue for the bus—it all revolved around questions: Were the boys evil? Sick? Inheritors of vicious tendencies? Socialized into beasts? Was it satanic, inhuman, or sociopathic for a child to kill another child? Or was it all too human?

Suddenly the old question—the Problem of Evil—was new again. Where does wickedness come from?

I had already been thinking about evil and the ways we can be astounded at the behavior of our peers, sometimes our kin, even when we have known them so well. I wondered, in the cases of aberration, whether (say) a Lizzie Borden had always been weird and dangerous, and locals had seen it in her eyes, or whether she'd formerly been a downright Pollyanna until something so severe happened to her that it actually changed her character. I wasn't interested in Lizzie Borden

herself. The question might be asked about anyone who commits what we might jointly agree is an act of evil: Hitler, the obvious example. Or those underage murdering lads. Are some people born with more of a capacity for wrongdoing than others, or does life brutalize some people beyond their endurance, and they snap?

This is a question that has no answer, yet to fail to ask it is irresponsible. We are obliged to think about our fellow humans. I hunted for a character that might serve as a literary exploration of this question. I don't remember exactly when it occurred to me that the Wicked Witch of the West was open for grabs, but in a desultory fashion I had toyed with the idea of writing about her for a couple of years. But when I first moved to England, someone had told me about a wonderful English novel called *Was*, involving an crazy old woman named Dorothy, and how her sad life might have inspired a traveling storyteller, L. Frank Baum. The novel was widely praised and I worried that Geoff Ryman, the author, might have invented in it something so wonderful about the Wicked Witch of the West that I would be daunted.

I procrastinated beginning my own novel, uncertain if the time was right, if I could dare such a monumental effort, until the week of my thirty-ninth birthday. This was June 1992, eight months before Jamie Bulger's death. I rented a car, slung *Was* in the back seat, and roared up the M6 to the Lake District. I rented a room in a nice B&B in Keswick and read Ryman's work with increasing admiration and anxiety. The morning I turned thirty-nine I finished the book with a sigh. Ryman had left the Witch alone. I was released to my own project, if I could find the heart, the brains, and the courage to do it.

Before heading back to London to start, I drove over to see Beatrix Potter's farm. It was a wet day, but English tourists were undeterred and the parking lot was full. I had to park far down a muddy lane and walk up to the farmhouse. On the way, I came across a single child's glove in the muck. I pulled it out. It was knit in bright colors of yarn and, like finger puppets, the tips of the fingers were stitched over with faces. I scraped the mud off it and looked more closely. The thumb showed the face of a little girl in pigtails. The pinky looked like the face of a black dog. Onto the tips of the three other fingers were crude representations of the Scarecrow, the Tin Woodman, the Lion.

I left the glove on a post so some child with a cold hand might have the chance of reclaiming it. I didn't need the glove. I had shaken hands with inspiration. Some child who cared for those characters as I cared for them was wandering about in the world—as we all are, a little lost, and in danger of coming face to face with wickedness. Some day he or she might grow up and want to read about it. I could present it in terms borrowed from the comfort and safety of childhood—when childhood is lucky enough to be safe and comfortable. I would have to get to work.

"Some child who cared for those characters as I cared for them was wandering about in the world—as we all are, a little lost, and in danger of coming face-to-face with wickedness."

Momento Mori

Adam Theron-Lee Rensch

Ask me how my father died and I'll say, "He fell and hit his head." I'll say, "It was a blood vessel that burst." I'll say, "It only took thirty seconds," because that's what the coroner said. I'll say, "I don't really know," because no one was there to see what happened, just my father, and he didn't bother to leave a note, as I'm sure he would have written, "Well I'll be dipped in shit." He was always one to make these kinds of remarks at an inappropriate time. Maybe he was dizzy, or maybe he dove headfirst. I only have images: the coffee table, the blood trail, the bile on the carpet. Sometimes I'll say his death is complicated, but this is only partly true—anything can be complicated, if you want it to be. It all depends what kind of story you want to tell. A tragedy. A mystery. A thriller. A romance. My father's death has been all of these. My favorite version is the comedy. "It's a funny story," I'll say, but no one who's heard it has ever laughed.

"I accidentally killed my father. I was trying to save him."

The story: When my stepmother was diagnosed with cancer, my father began drinking himself into a waking coma, a kind of slow-motion suicide. After she passed away, I began "taking care of him"—watching him while he slept, or while he paced around his apartment like a man planning his escape. I gave him money for the alcohol. Justified it with *I would too, if I were him*. His binges lasted for weeks, sometimes months, and then he'd call me from a pay phone on a street somewhere, telling me he was done, he was getting his life together.

During his last binge, he destroyed his apartment, the second one in the past year. He called me the night before he died and invited me over. "You need to see this," he said. Two things happened while I was there. The first is that he fell and hit his head. I can still see it—the way he was standing there, talking, how his eyes lit up and his body stiffened, the way he didn't even try to put his arms out as he hit the wall. He sat up afterwards, looked at me with a shrug, and said, "What is it? I'm fine." The other thing that happened was that, for the first time, I knew he wouldn't make it. In spite of this, perhaps because of it, I offered to help clean his apartment the following morning.

I arrived and found him asleep in a blanket of broken bottles. I woke him and he crawled to his soiled bed, nothing else in his room but a few dozen empty bottles and a broken stereo. I cleaned what I could, but after an hour I gave up. There was too much for one person, the bags kept breaking, the stench was unbearable. Just before I left, I remembered how he'd fallen the night before. Without thinking, I moved his furniture around, made a space so that, if he fell again, he wouldn't get hurt. An hour later, my father stumbled out of his bedroom, fell and hit his head on a coffee table I had moved to a corner. The impact burst something in his brain, and he died almost instantly.

I have remembered this moment many times: moving the table, looking back at the room, the way the morning light looked after a night of heavy snow. There lives a voice there now, in the house of my memory, the ghost of the last thing my father said to me. This ghost is a comedian. He knows how the story ends. "Be careful driving," he says, and then, with pitch-perfect delivery, a wry laugh, he gestures to where the body left him behind. "I'll be careful sitting."

The Secret Life of Parents

Elizabeth Gilbert

I must have been three years old because this happened in our old house, and we moved when I was four. I was upstairs, on the hallway carpet, on my belly, pushing a Barbie across the floor on her belly, as though she were a racecar. It was evening—after dinner, but before bedtime—and the household was slowly shutting down for the day. I could hear my parents moving about downstairs, making the mild noises of domestic life.

Then I heard my mother call to my father, who must have been in the basement, "John! I need to borrow you when you have a minute!"

It was, as I think anyone can plainly see, an innocuous exchange: a wife asking her husband for help with some mundane suburban chore. Still, hearing my mother's voice calling to my father like that filled me with the most eerie and unsettling realization—namely, that these two people, my parents, existed separately from me. It was the first time I'd noticed it. They had names (John and Carole) which they called each other privately—names which had nothing to do with their roles in my life as Mom and Dad. They spoke to each other even when I wasn't in the room, and moreover, they spoke about things that had nothing to do with me.

I wish there was a more subtle or elegant way for me to express this, but here's what I realized in that moment: I wasn't the center of the world. For heaven's sake, I wasn't even the center of this household.

I've heard it said that newborn infants believe the material world is an extension of their own bodies—that a baby can't tell where she ends and her mother (or her blanket or her family pet) begins. But I seem to have held on to that feeling of extreme universal connection long past infancy—until that evening in 1973, in fact, when I overheard my mother call to my father in a private moment, and I realized that these two people were not my limbs, after all. Along with that realization came, of course, a deep and sudden sense of being utterly alone.

You could say, I suppose, that this was my expulsion from Eden, the awakening of alienation's consciousness, the end of infancy's comforts. All of that is true enough, but all of that sounds pretty grim. Here's what it really was: The beginning of my life as a human being.

And beneath it all, here's how I felt: excited.

John Updike Sent Me a Fan Letter (Once)

Steve Almond

So I got this letter in the mail, one of those small, old-fashioned blue envelopes with a return address in Beverly Farms, Massachusetts. I was living in Somerville and trying to be a writer. I didn't know anyone in Beverly Farms. The only varieties of mail I received were bills and rejections from literary magazines.

Inside the blue envelope was a dainty letter that had been composed on a typewriter. In clear and careful prose, it praised an article I'd written for *Poets & Writers Magazine*. The signature at the bottom read: "John Updike."

I had several friends who knew of my admiration for Updike. I called them all immediately.

"Very funny," I said. "Very ha-ha-ha."

They pretended to have no idea what I was talking about.

I inspected the envelope again. The postmark was from the Beverly Farms post office, which meant one of my friends would have had to travel to that town to mail the letter. My friends were certainly capable of pranking me. But they were way too lazy to make that kind of effort.

Ipso facto, John Updike had written me a fan letter.

I'm not sure I can articulate how inspiring I found this. I was, at best, a literary fledgling. John Updike was, uh, John Updike. The idea that he'd taken the time to read something I'd written and been sufficiently impressed to track down my address and send me a letter—it was sort of like Michael Jordan showing up at a public playground to tell the worst guy there that he had a nice shot. That's how it felt, anyway.

I've managed to publish a few books in the decade since I received Updike's letter. I can now see more clearly how generous he was being. He certainly had better things to do with his time.

What I'm saying is that Updike, without necessarily intending to, was teaching me something: that it's one of our jobs as writers to be unnecessarily generous—especially if we manage to win a little notice. And that the point of joining the community of artists is to appreciate, not to be appreciated. It's easy to forget this, given the disregard most of us feel we suffer. Envy comes a lot more naturally.

I keep Updike's letter in the top drawer of my desk. Not so I can show it off to friends—though I did plenty of that in the old days—but so I don't forget the real lesson.

C-Listed

Mary Elizabeth Williams

I t's not the diagnosis that changes your life, though that's quite a corker too.

One lovely August morning, you are just doing what you usually do, banging away at a computer keyboard, desperately trying to make a deadline, when the phone rings. Five minutes later, you are a different person.

There hadn't been any ominous buildup, not really. No strange pains, no lengthy series of illnesses. It had just been a persistent little nub on the head, a scab that wouldn't heal. You figured you'd scraped yourself up somehow in the course of summertime's swimming and playing with your daughters, and maybe it had gotten infected. You had dragged your heels about going to the dermatologist, and had barely blinked even when she sucked in her breath and said, "That looks like skin cancer." Skin cancer. "Big deal," you had thought. "If I have to come back and have something scraped off, so be it." At least it wasn't on your face. You dutifully submitted to a biopsy and thought nothing else of it.

Then six days later, everything changes. You've had phone calls from doctors before. You've had the suspicious cells checked out;

> *And it's both comforting and terrible to begin to fathom that the day-to-day does not grind to a halt simply because you now might be in huge trouble here."*

you've heard the "we need to do more tests" message. You sigh when you recognize the number on your caller ID, irritated at the interruption in you train of thought. Then voice on the other end says, "It's Dr. Rosen. We got your labs back and I'm sorry, it's malignant."

You know now that there's a reason they use the word "shattering" to describe certain experiences. It's not so much that you break apart—it's that you split into so many little pieces. The part of yourself that is slowly absorbing the word "malignant" is fighting for control with the part that's screaming, "Your boss is going to be so pissed that you're running behind on your work here." The part that's realizing, "I guess this means I could die pretty soon" is very busy, but no more so than the part that's wondering, "Did she say I have to go to Sloan-Kettering *tomorrow*? But who will pick up the kids at camp?"

Your brain whirs in a hundred directions at once, and very few of them are "I am a person with cancer." You have not yet put on the garb of sick person. Why should you? You don't feel any different than you did at breakfast; you don't notice any sudden uptick in your cancerousness. There are too many practical matters—deadlines and errands—to attend to anyway. And it's both comforting and terrible to begin to fathom that the day-to-day does not grind to a halt simply because you now might be in huge trouble here. Your meeting tomorrow with your brand new oncologist to talk about your "treatment" isn't just a life-or-death necessity—it's a damn inconvenience.

You don't know yet what your treatment entails. The only times in your life up to this point you've ever worn a hospital gown, you were delivering babies. You will learn, and soon, about what the cells in your body have been up to. You will sit in waiting rooms with quiet, hairless people and their scared-shitless-looking loved ones. You will cry oceans of tears. You will find out who are your friends, and who are not. You will experience unimaginable pain and alarming scars and the profoundest, purest love. You will learn exactly what you are made of, and you will, in time, receive puzzled looks from people when you tell them you're grateful this happened. But not today.

Instead, now you put down the phone and stare numbly at your computer screen. You have words to write. You have people who depend on you. And none of them has any idea yet of your condition. You're still a stranger to it yourself. So you sit back for a few seconds and take deep breaths, savoring the languorous beauty of your secret.

As far as the rest of the world is concerned, you're still you. You are the same healthy and normal person they laugh with at the movies, they tease at work, they run to with scraped knees, they kiss in the dark. But that person is leaving the building. She will be replaced by someone who for a while can make her friends burst into tears at the very sight of her, who will inspire well-wishers to gawk at her scars while making small talk, who must now add one more self-description to her name under "writer," "mother," and "bigmouthed Jersey girl." Now, though, you have work to finish. So your boss pings you suddenly to nudge, "Are you almost finished?"

"Almost," you type back. "I just got off the phone." And though you still don't quite believe the words yourself, you get your first crack at practicing saying them. You pick up the cloak, and you put it on. It feels awkward and strange, but you can already tell how frighteningly well it fits. "I have cancer," you write.

And your new life begins.

Breast cancer diagnosis woke me up.
—*Christine Kunert*

SHE HID CANCER, DIED SUDDENLY TODAY.
—*Dave Boyce*

My humor kills my cancer cells.
—*Maria Leopoldo*

Cancer: War husband didn't return from.
—*Jo-Ellen Balogh*

Escaped narcissist; survived cancer;
found paradise.
—*Gail Tobey*

Breast cancer: zero. My future: won.
—*Amy Bowker*

Polio, cancer, Crohn's and still here.
—*Sylvia Smith*

After cancer, I became a semicolon.
—*Anthony R. Cardno*

WAITED OUT CANCER; YOU SAID 'BYE.
—*Joe Carlson*

Cancer has become a six-letter memoir.
—*Beverly Head*

5RLG375

Chris Sacca

On June 5, 2007, I watched a man get shot.

Standing outside my apartment building in San Francisco, I had just two hours before a flight to the UK and was typing a rushed packing list on my BlackBerry. Suddenly I heard two loud, distinct pops. I can't say they sounded unfamiliar, but I dismissed them. The potential to hear gunshots on a Monday, in my neighborhood, was so out of the realm of possibility, my brain searched for other explanations. A car backfiring? Fireworks?

Any attempt to reasonably explain away what my ears had just heard was undermined by the report from my eyes. I was looking across the street at an Asian guy in his thirties clutching desperately at his loins as his legs gave out and he crumbled to the pavement. If there was any doubt remaining about what just had taken place, a silver Chrysler 300 fleeing the scene squealed its tires as it streaked toward me. Holy shit.

The shooter, a black male behind the wheel, was pinned at the intersection of 3rd and Townsend. Stuck in the right hand lane, the traffic heading up 3rd Street left him no immediate options to escape. A large semitruck was in the lane to his left, further boxing him in and simultaneously providing me cover.

Thus, I made my move and sprinted toward the car. I rolled my body along the edge of the trailer until I was able to catch the full license plate number, just before he found a window to spin out across the intersection toward the Embarcadero. It wasn't until much later that I started to digest that, at one point, I had been a car length from an attempted murderer. Thank goodness the insanity of that adjacency didn't occur to me in the moment. Instead, I had a singular obsession—write down that plate number before I forgot it.

By now there was shouting coming at me from all sides. "Hey, get down! Get down!" "Someone get that license plate number!" "Watch out!" I steadied my hands just long enough to etch the digits onto my mobile screen: "5RLG375."

The remaining items on my packing list soon read:

Socks (blue and black for Oxford)
Baseball cap
Jacket
***Harper's* and *Atlantic* mags**
Take out trash
Pull kite, harness, and lines from truck
5RLG375

Plate number in hand, I dialed 911—busy signal, of course—and ran back to aid the victim. He was face down on the pavement, one arm splayed out above his head, a dike guiding the fluorescent red blood as it left him on its dash for the gutter.

The few of us standing there were helpless, not knowing what to do. They didn't cover drive-bys and massive trauma in the CPR course I once took. Then a kind man in his mid-forties placed his hand on the victim's back and repeated with inspired but dubitable confidence that everything would be all right. A police officer who happened to be nearby rushed over on foot. I gave him the plate number, and immediately after his call went out we could hear the echoes of sirens firing up across the city.

The cop rolled the downed man onto his back, revealing his injuries. There was so much blood. So much pain, panic, and fear in his face. The paramedics responded with feverish urgency. They tore off the man's clothes, working almost spastically to clean and stabilize his wound. One announced that the bullet was still lodged in him while another declared he was losing too much blood.

This was interrupted intermittently by the cop's crackling radio. There was a shared but virtually silent celebration when we learned that the shooter had been cornered and taken into custody near the Bay Bridge. Notions of civil justice, despite what the movies may tell you, feel quite hollow while peering down at a man struggling for his life.

It took a few minutes before a bystander noticed a strange copper crumb at his feet—it was one of the two bullets fired, the other still burrowed deep within the victim's body. This errant projectile was rejected by the building's steel and concrete façade, leaving a small dent in the wall.

I crossed the street to my home and hoped a return to packing my bags might pause the gory movie playing on a loop in my head. Then I noticed for the first time how sweaty I was, my shirt clinging to my body and my brow dripping. I distracted myself by loading playlists onto my iPod and combing the house for some miniature toiletries approved to fit in the TSA-prescribed plastic bag. Within an hour, the airplane mercifully whisked me far away, my nails digging into the armrests as I was engulfed by the isolating din of the pressurized cabin. Yet no matter how far I traveled on that trip, a piercing anxiety was my unrelenting companion. Despair, confusion, and rage joined me as well.

Years later I still can't delete that macabre scene from my mind, and my loose ends remain untied. The victim's name was never released, though I later found out that he lived. I learned of the trial only after it was wrapped, and the shooter's confession earned him a life sentence. And I never got to know any of the other witnesses.

So it is that I am alone every June when I walk to the scene of the crime, crouch down, and run my fingers back and forth over the pock mark on the wall where the second bullet hit, wishing aloud that it could answer any one of the questions that make me cry as I type this.

My Blue Sticky

Fiona Maazel

I am a text person. I communicate best in text and almost not at all in speech. The words come out, but they rarely have anything to do with the feelings I sustain inside. I do not claim this pathology for myself alone nor do I find its fallout all that tragic. I am not duplicitous so much as withdrawn, which becomes a problem only in situations that require emotional presence, and for which times I've developed a solution. A game I call Text/Subtext. It goes like this: Say you're having dinner with a friend, lover, parent. The banter is: my day and yours. But the feelings are otherwise: I am so sad. I want to do unspeakable things to your body. Please don't die. And so: If there's gain to be had in the release of these secrets but no way to do so in speech, out comes the pen and paper. And a passing of notes whose dialogue doesn't subvert so much as complement the one I had going already. My day and yours. How 'bout those Mets.

Many years ago, I was talking to, let's call this person Q. We were laughing about something or other—we often did—until the bleakness of my inner life came tumbling out on a blue sticky note, which I still keep in my wallet. Back then, I thought this exchange meant I wouldn't be alone anymore. I was wrong, insofar as we're all alone, but never mind. It meant something big to me in the moment.

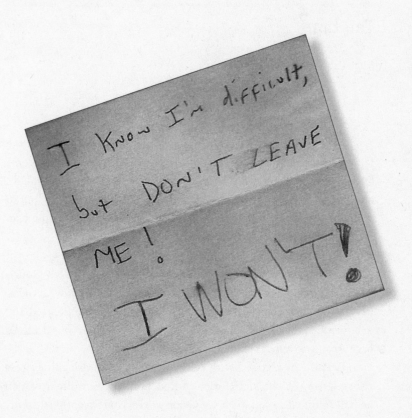

Lives

Tao Lin

The first day of my dad's trial the judge fell asleep. One of the jurors also fell asleep. The judge was startled awake when a lawyer shouted "objection!" My mom told me these things. My dad's lawyer had advised my brother and me not to attend the trial, but to attend the day of sentencing—reasoning, I thought, that it might elicit sympathy from the judge and jury.

On the sentencing day, I got out early from my Chinese class at New York University and rode the N train to the Brooklyn Courthouse. My mom and brother were already there and I sat with them. My dad was with his lawyer. He waved at us, seeming focused and in control, and I thought that he was probably very nervous. I waved back, trying to appear calm.

My dad was charged with releasing false and misleading press releases to raise the stock price of his company, Surgilight, which he had founded to sell his laser vision-correction inventions. In my opinion he made—at worst—a few semantic mistakes. I felt strongly that he wasn't capable of intentionally harming or taking advantage of anyone. He never used the word "love," never really hugged or kissed my brother or me on his own volition, but he did, for example, keep employees on the payroll even when his company was failing and there was no work to do, and he gave loans to anyone who asked, even when he knew he probably wouldn't be repaid.

But the jury had found him guilty and now the judge was going to decide his sentence. I stared at the judge's face and thought about how he'd fallen asleep. When he said seventy months, I calculated it as five years and stopped thinking. I didn't feel much emotion until my dad was given a chance to speak for the last time. He read from a letter he had prepared: "In prison I cannot make any further contributions to society. In prison I am useless. . . . I will fight to the end for my reputation, innocence, and name." While reading he twitched in a way that seemed both intentional and uncontrollable, as if physically struggling against something, though he was standing alone in an open area near the front of the courtroom. The prosecuting lawyer interrupted, and my dad said, "Come on! Will you give me a chance to talk? You've been lying this whole time!" His face was red and his body was trembling. Watching this I felt a dizzying confusion, like the moment between falling and recovering, but sustained. I felt like crying.

After the sentencing I looked at my brother. He seemed catatonic with emotion. My mom's eyes were wet and red and she was smiling, weakly and awkwardly, like a stroke patient.

That was in April. In July, my mom drove my dad to a federal correctional complex in Coleman, Florida. Over the next couple of months, my brother and I wrote letters to him from New York City. My mom visited twice a week, driving an hour from her home in Orlando.

In letters, my dad said he was content, even happy. He liked the food. He was teaching Chinese to a class of inmates. He had submitted two new patents, written half a dozen ophthalmology papers, and used his PhD in physics to help another inmate write a chapter of a novel involving flying saucers.

Two months after going to prison my dad signed one of his letters to me "love, Dad." It was the first time he had ever mentioned "love" to me. I examined the handwriting and cried. I had always known my dad as a stoic mad-scientist, someone who found it difficult or impossible to express intimate affection toward other people. When calling home from business trips he always asked how the dogs were—never my brother, mom, or me. A few weeks later my mom e-mailed me saying my dad had written her a letter. "A real letter, the first one in twenty years." In the letter my dad said he had become too focused on business and had forgotten to care for my mom, for people. "This is the real dad I knew a long time ago and I love the changes in him," my mom's e-mail said. "I was so moved that I cried for a long time."

When I read my mom's e-mail I cried also.

Teachable Moment

Bill Ayers, with Ryan Alexander-Tanner

'd been arrested at an antiwar sit-in in 1965, and I'd spent ten days in jail where I met the husband of the founder of a small freedom school affiliated with the Black Freedom Movement. I walked out of jail and into my first teaching job at the Children's Community, a beautiful child-centered space with a big agenda: "An Experiment in Freedom and Integration." Our buttons read: "Kids are only newer people."

The moment came near the end of my first year in a classroom, a year in which a group of kids taught me all I really needed to know to become a good teacher (although goodness in teaching is a life-long pursuit). There they were, humming along on a project that engaged their minds, activated their spirits, moved their bodies, and built the classroom community. I never wanted to leave that magic behind.

From that day on, education has been linked in my mind to the twin pillars of enlightenment and liberation. Teaching is ethical work, and I learned early on that the fundamental message of the teacher is this: You can change your life; you can change the world.

Disappointment

Nevenka Kurjakovic

My mom has been waiting several hours for me to show up for lunch at her carriage house apartment only two blocks from my office. In anticipation she reheats the red-skinned potatoes and meat loaf ("several times") that she prepared ("all morning"). I smell the familiar meal as I yank open the door to climb the stairs at the back of the garage. "Mama *tu sam*," I call up from the bottom step. I am here. To which she shakes her head at the top of the stairs and utters one of her favorite admonitions. Then she welcomes me into her warm, sunlit kitchen.

There is one place setting at the table waiting for me. I sit down. She stands. Apron on, pants and sleeves rolled up, she busies herself turning on the gas under the teakettle several times before it catches.

"I'm sorry I'm late, I had a lot to finish up," I lie. My lateness is not so much because of work at the office as that I dread the visits. A lifetime worth of unfulfilled needs and failed expectations has left me with feelings too raw at age forty-five, and no matter how I have tried, or how she has tried, eventually some comment stings and flares up emotions. And it always ends the same way: me feeling powerless and misunderstood, wrong and guilty.

"Would you like tea or coffee, dear?" she offers.

"Anything hot. If you have lemon, I'll take some tea."

Mixed tea bag tags hang over the top of the tin teakettle. She's reheating that too for the nth time. Lipton Decaf, Chamomile, Red Rose—chemical engineer turned culinary pioneer—I am not in the mood for another one of her experiments.

"Here, put a napkin over your nice slacks, darling." She does it for me then stands by the stove stirring the potatoes, adjusting the flame, asking the same questions I've already answered. As usual she's not listening. She fills my cup halfway. I add a dollop of sugar and squeeze a few drops out of a lemon half, and wrap my cold hands around the lukewarm mug. *I wanted something hot,* I think to myself, as I taste the tepid tea.

"How is it, darling?" She looks over at me, and even though I don't say anything, her smile is cut off and now she resembles a chastised child.

Disappointment spreads from her face to her shoulders, and I know that she knows what I am thinking. She looks at me with sad eyes and, holding on to the bottom of her apron, says, "That's how it has always been with us, isn't it?" No judgment. Just fact.

This is the moment that changes my relationship with my mom. *How sad for her to give her only daughter all of her best and it's never good or right. How sad for both people.* I eat the meal she made for me, wipe my face, and as I get up to leave I say, "Mom, it was delicious! Thank you." And I mean it. I hug her, and she looks up at me and smiles.

Divine Intervention

Dan Goggin

Whent my first *Nunsense* show opened off-Broadway in 1985 at a historic little theater on a charming but rarely traveled street in Greenwich Village, I had no idea how important walk-up business was to the success of a show. Audiences came and loved the show, but not in sizable numbers. By the end of the first month we were running in the "red" and the theater rescinded our

lease. We couldn't believe they would do that when we were struggling to stay alive. Little did we know that it would be the "moment" that eventually would make us a hit.

The scuttlebutt was that a theater located at a main intersection had a play that was about to close. I felt we couldn't stop trying to keep *Nunsense* running since audiences were responding so fantastically. So we borrowed twenty thousand dollars and moved to the theater at the very busy intersection. The first night we did twenty-five hundred dollars in walk-up business!

The move literally saved the show from extinction. Had the original theater let us stay on, we probably would have just faded away trying. That move happened twenty-five years ago. Since then, there have been over eight thousand productions of *Nunsense* and its seven sequel musicals around the world grossing more than five hundred million dollars. "Divine Intervention" truly changed my life and the lives of hundreds of future "nuns."

Poem for the Moment

Matthew Zapruder

at certain moments I lift my head

and remember my backyard

which is not really mine but I have paid

rent so I get to look at it here

in the most touristy neighborhood

of this sleepy city connected

to everything by bridges so maps

make it look from above

like a lopsided starfish

I always forget how close I live to the water

and in those moments I manage
to become incrementally less
than fully distracted by obligations
I cannot even remember
gradually having allowed to become
the terrible geometric honeycomb
of my day and therefore am able
to reach my hand
up to open the venetian blinds
and usually see not much happening
maybe a crow pecking at one of the plants
in rows the beautiful gardener
my landlord has hired to create
vegetables out of nothing
but soil and seeds and water
and whatever music
she listens to through her headphones
sometimes I see her do a funny dance
right before she turns on the hose
or a small mouse running furiously
from under one plant to beneath
the old blue chair
where it's safe and shadowy
and I know in just a few months
we will get married

underneath a tree whose leaves

say beautiful worried lovers

no matter what anyone says to you

when we rustle we are saying believe us

though we know you know leaves don't speak

and I also know some day

or maybe it has already passed

there will be one moment

I won't even notice when I am halfway

through everything I will do

and I will have started

to wear my body like an old machine

that wants nothing not even

the long gone intimation of celerity

or something else that cannot be recalled

Mr. Criche

Dave Eggers

When I was a junior in high school, I had an English teacher named Mr. Criche. He was universally regarded as a master teacher; he was the head of the department, and looked like it. He wore wire-rimmed glasses, tweed sport coats, and, if I remember correctly, there were suede patches on the elbows of these sport coats. I remember trying to impress him by bringing *As I Lay Dying* to class, even though it wasn't assigned reading. (It didn't make any sense to me at the time . . . but anyway.) We read *Macbeth* that year, and after procrastinating till the night before it was due, I wrote a paper about the play—it was the first paper I typed on a typewriter—and turned it in the next day. I got a good grade on it, and below the grade Mr. Criche wrote, "Sure hope you become a writer." That was it. Just those six words. It was the first time someone had indicated in any way that writing was a career option for me. We'd never had any writers in our family line, and we didn't know any writers personally, even distantly, so it didn't seem something available to me. But over the next ten years, I thought often about those six words Mr. Criche wrote. And even when I was discouraged by some instructors in college, Mr. Criche's words always came back to me and gave me strength.

Since then, I've realized the power that a teacher can provide. I had attentive parents but they would never have suggested that career path to me. But a teacher can sometimes open doors for you. A teacher can say, "Have you ever thought about being a biochemist?" And given their expertise in that subject matter, they're in a position to point the way to a certain route—more so than a parent who, say, might not know much about biochemistry. So now, when I teach my own high school classes, I always think of the power of Mr. Criche's words, and I try to measure and use my own carefully, knowing the impact they might have.

"That was it. Just those six words. It was the first time someone had indicated in any way that writing was a career option for me."

Cornrows

Lori Sabian

Wanna come over after school?"

As a seven-year-old girl, this was the pinnacle of social success. A coveted invitation from the ruling girl group for after school mischief was like gold bullion. Like a typical seven-year-old girl, my mind raced with the kinds of fun we could have. Barbies? Dress up? Some elaborate fantasy with knights, the Wizard of Oz and princesses?

Finally, school let out and the four of us trekked to her house. It smelled of Keebler cookies, cocoa butter, and fried chicken. It was small in all the places my house was big. It was dark in all the places my house was light. We ate Twinkies, Pop-Tarts, and cookies with little elfin men, which in my house would have been incinerated. Such riches of junk food I had only peered at in the supermarket or on television commercials. I didn't think real people lived this way, until that day. I felt so lucky to be included. And ready to fully participate.

Then it was decided that our afternoon project would be hair. Specifically, the braiding, greasing, and cornrowing of hair. The four of us took to the task with gusto. The jar of Vaseline came out. Assorted colored rubber bands, barrettes, and ribbons were on display.

Three of us working on one girl produced complicated designs with braids and parts. Occasionally, a tender-headed yelp would bubble out of the girl being made over. We would roll our eyes and laugh about her poor scalp, slap on some more Vaseline and continue.

My turn was last. It became clear very quickly my hair did not respond as expected. More Vaseline was applied. More rubber bands came out and still it did not obey. We tried our very best to keep my slippery straight hair bound by tiny braids. All four of us could not identify where we went wrong. Finally, after exhausting a jar of Vaseline, we gave up. The four of us decided I had a rare combination of tender scalp and brown hair. It was lethal for braiding, but still fun to play with. We decided to try again another time. Doing hair together was a rousing success.

I got home in time for a quick dinner and a long bath. My mother and I spent about fifteen minutes washing out the Vaseline. As I was giving a glowing retelling of the afternoon, I began to realize how different I was from my playmates. I was a different hair color. I was a different eye color. I didn't have pictures of Jesus in the kitchen. I didn't have special ribbons to wear on Sunday. Deeper than food and family, I was a different skin color. In short, I realized I was a white Jewish girl and not black like my girlfriends. No one had ever pointed this out to me before. At that moment of insight, I felt an odd mixture of confusion, disappointment, and awe.

This is the moment, and its combination of emotions, that fueled a lifelong pursuit of education, collaboration, and inclusion. Because of this realization, differences became a way to connect with others. Differences became the way to open up relationships between children and adults in classrooms. Differences changed into profound learning experiences outside of the planned curriculum. My most basic and yet more core understanding of people came about through failed cornrows. And I still want the cornrows.

Dancing, in Green, to Ravel

Ellen O'Connell

The ballet was called *Serenade*, and I danced it with a tall blond named David, who could watch a dance once and memorize exactly what he had to do. It was the kind of ballet I was perfect for, without Martha Graham contractions or Balanchine pirouettes, without unitards or gongs. It was pure Ashton or Macmillan, something that could have been danced in France or Russia fifty years ago. It was something that my dead grandmother could have seen as a young woman, when she knew Margot Fonteyn, who came over, kicked off her shoes and danced in my grandmother's backyard at a cocktail party.

"You run over to me and I'll do the rest," David said. "Just leave it to me." I stood in black stirrup tights and pointe shoes off to the side of the mirrored studio and waited.

To begin, he crossed the stage in a diagonal: walking, reaching, uncoiling from pirouettes into arabesques. The string adagio matched the quiet regularity of rain just outside. I ran forward and stopped, repeating the steps just danced by David. He danced right behind me, not quite touching unless I leaned so far that he needed to catch me, or I turned so much that his hands would stop my waist, spinning me until I unfolded and caught the music with my body. My steps were a prologue to his. We were like two paired birds, plunging in a compact series, never varying our distance from each other in the sky.

"Stage right!" The choreographer directed. "Downstage! Look at her. Keep your eyes on him as he runs from you. Now run to him."

There was one lift that terrified me most, that I spent the whole first half dreading, and the second half recovering from. When the lift went well, we looked at each other afterwards, as though only just noticing one has dark eyelashes and the other an Adam's apple that drops when he swallows.

"That was my fault," David would say to the choreographer when it didn't go as well. He took the blame every time, as male dancers are perhaps taught to do. Time and time again, when a lift would go wrong, or the timing was not matched, he called the fault his and then privately told me the things I should do differently.

The music resumed. We retraced the steps that led me to him. He ran away, he looked back, I ran to him. When I jumped, it didn't make sense that he would have continued and left me behind. I held my breath for that moment when I had no control over gravity and everything was left to David and the ballet and all the training I ever had. Then the floor grew and grew until my face hit it, and my shoulder, and my hip that jutted from my black tights like some rare bird. As I rolled on my back, I felt a fate worse than gravity.

There is a measure of trust involved in allowing someone else to lift you so high, and while I was falling I trusted still, expecting he'd find a way to plunge down and catch me before I met the bottom. It crossed my mind that I never wanted to do that lift again. I gave up right there, on the ground. I don't remember the fall or what it felt like to land. I don't remember how it hurt, just that it hurt.

The music kept playing as I lay there. David and the choreographer rushed to my side. I lay on my back with my legs pulled to my chest, and wide-eyed people stood around me and spoke quietly, the way they do when they try to pretend that everything is as it should be. I looked up at a white ceiling and thought about my mother's face, and how her cheekbones were so perfect that I never wanted to look away. I thought about the perfume she wore when she went to the opera and wondered who made it.

I couldn't walk into the hospital that night, so they wheeled me in. There were three x-rays, backlit on the wall, and the doctor pointed to them as though I might recognize something foreign. Mostly I saw the tree branches of my ribs, white and blurred.

"Here's the fracture in the lower spine. L4 and L5 have compressed here and here as well, so you have bone on bone, and the fluid has begun to leak." He used a pen to point, but to me it looked just like what it was supposed to.

"Here is the first fracture in the spine, and down here is another one." He traced them in a smooth arc. "If you were a normal weight," the doctor continued, "this probably would not have happened. Try to gain a few pounds, OK?"

People understand physical pain in a way they don't understand anything else. There is a crack, a rupture, a doctor. There is a pill, or a handful of them, exercise, restrictions. Somatic pain is the easiest to explain, and the easiest to dance through. Pain like that knows your name, and it doesn't wait for you.

They told me when I first broke my back that it was unlikely I would dance again, but for a few more years I thought I could outrun something always nipping at my heels. My body needed to catch up to where my mind was, and my mind was stuck on choreography. I didn't have long, but I had youth that wasn't yet used up. So I kept performing, and when I was lucky I stayed one step ahead of the pain, but more often the pain outdanced me.

The last time I danced onstage, I only half realized it. All that mattered was how much I could defy gravity that night.

Fluke

Danny Davis

After winning the final Winter Dew Tour stop of the season in late January, snowboarder Danny Davis celebrated by going out drinking with friends and then taking out an ATV, which he crashed, ending his season. He woke up in ICU at a Salt Lake City hospital with broken vertebrae and a broken pelvis. Two weeks earlier, his best friend and Olympic hopeful Kevin Pearce suffered a traumatic brain injury while practicing in the half-pipe. When Davis was injured, Pearce was still in a coma at a nearby hospital in Salt Lake City.

The moment I woke up in the hospital, I knew I was hurt bad. I also knew I'd blown it beyond belief. I knew any Olympic opportunity was gone, everything I'd worked so hard for. But for some reason, that didn't matter because I was alive and I knew I was lucky. There are bigger things than the Olympics. I was so close to being paralyzed, but I could walk. And I was alive. I started trying to figure out where I was, and I remembered that I had won the Dew Tour contest the night before and that we had gone to a party. Then I remembered

Kevin was still in a coma from his injury two weeks before. Once I found out why I was in the hospital, because I'd wrecked an ATV, I felt bad that I got injured being an idiot, but I was alive and awake and going to be able to walk. And Kevin got injured pushing his limits and pushing the sport and we didn't know if he would wake up or how he would recover. It was a big wake-up call for me. Before the accident, I was partying with no realization of how much I was drinking. Every time I drank, it was just as much as I could. I never thought, "How many beers have I had?" That has changed, so has the way I hang out with my friends and the way I party.

I think things through more now. I think about whether the risk is worth it, even in snowboarding. I never did that before. I also learned some things happen for no reason. I used to believe everything had a purpose. Sure, I learned from my accident, but there was no reason for what happened to Kevin. He was working so hard to make the Olympic team and he didn't have an ounce of mean blood in his body. But that still happened to him. There is no reason something that bad should happen to such a good person. In that moment when I woke up, I also thought, *I am still here, so I must have something more to do on this earth.* Not as if I am going to save the world. But I felt that I was kept around for a reason. I get the feeling I have quite a bit more to do while I am alive. I just don't know what that is yet.

Persephone

Micah Toub

She was down by my outstretched legs, on her knees and bent over forwards. As if she was praying. In fact, she was praying. She was weeping, too, over the wreckage of my body. She had long dark hair, olive skin, and was wearing high heels and a tight black dress that showed her thighs. She was the most stunningly sexy woman that I had ever seen, that had ever touched me.

Later, I would realize her tears were not just for me; they were also for whatever it was she'd been running from in that stolen car. But it didn't matter on the sidewalk, surrounded by all the people standing and staring with numb interest; her despair calmed me and I exhaled and even smiled as I gazed into the cloudless sunny sky. She turned her wet cheeks toward me and asked if I was okay and told me she was sorry, but to be honest, I had never felt so alive in my life.

Trash

Rigoberto González

We didn't have a washing machine in our house, so at week's end my task was to take the laundry down the street to my aunt's. My mother would walk over later in the afternoon to do the wash.

The clothes were packed tightly into a trash bag, which I balanced on the handle bars. Usually I didn't complain about the chore. I was ten, and the ride was an escape from our crowded little house with its squeaky stairs and broken refrigerator door. But this time I made the trip reluctantly because of what I'd overheard the week before: "Every time there's less for that woman to wash," my aunt had said to her neighbor, "because their rags have more holes."

En route, I was distracted by the echo of the insult and by the truth that ours was the poorest branch of the family tree. So when I came upon a dumpster, it seemed quite logical, mechanical even, that I drop the lumpy trash bag into its huge square mouth. Dissatisfied with the quickness of the gesture, I rolled back around to empty the contents over the spoils of fly-infested waste.

How pleasantly surprised I was when I thought that my

mother had decided finally to toss out our old clothing with all its embarrassments—tears, snags and stains that never came off. And a second later, how devastated I was that I had deliberately thrown away the clothing we were going to have to wear next week. I stood on my toes at the edge of the dumpster as I pulled at my shirts, my mother's bra, my father's pants, all the while dreading what else my aunt would have to say about our rotten smell, our additional layer of filth.

I knew then I would never grow up to be poor.

Gonzo Girl

Cheryl Della Pietra

I have an Ivy League diploma on my wall and an ice strainer in my hand. It's 1992, and I'm a recent graduate living in New York, trying to work for a magazine. Any magazine will do. In the meantime, I'm pouring drinks that involve too much blue curaçao and Malibu rum for the bridge-and-tunnel crowd at a blues bar on Bleecker Street in Greenwich Village. I'm not too proud for this job, but some days I just want to take our ice pick and stab it in my eye. I live on the top floor of a fifth-floor walk-up in Soho, which you could do in 1992, making next to nothing, if you had a roommate, which I do. We have no TV. Our Mac Classic computer was stolen during a break-in while I was sleeping. No one we know has a cell phone, or an e-mail address. Our cheap entertainment consists of going to the all-night deli at all hours dressed in some version of our pajamas and getting a bottle of Budweiser in a brown paper bag. We smoke cigarettes and drink the Bud in the park at Thompson and Spring.

That February, my roommate tells me our friend Dan, who has a job interning at *Rolling Stone*, says Hunter S. Thompson is looking for an "assistant." What this means I have no idea. I'll find out later when I'm drinking scotch in a hot tub surrounded by seven key lime pies and a gun; right now I only know that whatever it involves will be better than shaking another Long Island Iced Tea. It will be better than one more "informational interview" at Conde Nast, where I have failed the fucking typing test twice. It will be amazing. If I get it.

I write a letter. Not a long one, but not one out of any career book. It is an honest letter. One in which I'm sure it comes through that I feel like a pathetic underachiever in this mean, closed-up city. One in which I tell him how much I really like his work. One that does not ignore the fact that I'm ripe, ready, and very much able to mix a drink. It's a long shot, but it feels good. I don't want to get this job any other way—by lying or embellishing how qualified I am. I'm twenty-two for God's sake. I'm not Tina Brown. We both know that. I fax the letter, because that is what you do in 1992.

I'm often up until two, but almost never three. And even though at this hour I've slept through hotel fire alarms, the phone jars me awake. The voice could be a prank, but it's too random, and too much as I've imagined from what I've read. It's a barky mumble, at once shy and demanding.

"Can you get out here tomorrow?"

"I'm sorry?" I say, sitting up.

"This is Hunter Thompson. You want this job? Get out here tomorrow."

"Tomorrow." I say this as statement, not a question. Not an are-you-out-of-your-fucking head indictment. You don't become the father of Gonzo journalism by waiting. You make things happen. If I hesitate, I'll chicken out. Or worse, he'll sense my trepidation and wake up the next candidate on his list. "Of course I can."

"Great. She'll call in the morning. I liked your letter."

"Thanks."

And then the click. We were done.

The way I got this job—by not hesitating, by saying yes—will come back to me in the ensuing months as I live and work beside the master of such sentiments. I'll learn that you can live by these rules. Indeed, what's the point otherwise?

I lie back in bed. I could think about details right now, like what I will wear tomorrow and who will cover my next shift at the bar. I could be scared or triumphant. But I'm neither. I roll over and wrap the covers to my chin like a child on Christmas Eve, content, anticipating. I sleep so soundly, ten fire alarms couldn't wake me.

I don't know I'm about to be thrown directly into the fire.

Rimshot

Josh Axelrad

Four days shy of the one-month anniversary of the World Trade Center attacks, the phone rang in the room where Clem and I sat with controllers in our hands. We were playing Grand Theft Auto. Violence, in a game, remained fun. In Brooklyn times were strange. The reek of dead metal from across the East River still lingered. No one could imagine asserting what later would become such a commonplace: that 9/11 represented an apex and the best day of many lives. Perverse, you might say, but it's true.

Kooky, raging hungers produce weird attitudes. Just before the turn of the millennium, four years out of college, I'd grown so starved for reality I'd commenced a new career playing blackjack professionally with a card-counting team, and the primary motivation—aside from income and the chance to fly between American towns on incredible jets on a tax-deductible basis—was flight in a different sense, flight from our pursuers, from bosses and the armed guards who routinely threw us out of their casinos. In flight, in fear or in terror you got embodiment, your heart gave way to a present moment expansive and absolute; everything abstract went ignored, and you never had a question as to value: you ran.

Clem's phone was a landline. Inside was an actual bell. Or some metal bell-like device. It rang physically. He paused the game, rising unsteadily on his humorous, gaunt legs, and went to see what was the matter.

"I understand," he said after a pause. "Thank you." He hung up the phone.

His expression was faux-somber as he strode back toward the couch. He raised a significant eyebrow and nodded at me, sighing. "We're bombing Afghanistan," Clem said.

I hadn't seen that coming. It was Sunday and we were stoned.

"That was Burt?" I said.

"Yeah."

Burt worked, menially, at the *New York Times*. Having gotten the report on the commencement of the war he had to tell someone, and Clem was his choice. It was incongruous, but, to us, fitting.

We weren't exactly the Joint Chiefs of Staff. But before the story even hit the *Times* website, Clem and I were right on top of it. Perhaps even the president or Dick Cheney hadn't gotten the official word yet.

"Ready?" Clem said.

We continued our game. The feeling of lightheartedness never did subside, but as the evening grew late I was bothered. Clem, Burt, and I were clowns. We're bombing Afghanistan—rimshot! Rather than the vigorous humor that affirms life by expressing transcendence of suffering, ours was nihilistic. It negated all things, pain as much as life as much as love, by treating them identically, with scorn.

This was our essential attitude, or mine, and I resented it. I'd been waiting for the change that the attacks seemed to augur. The intervening weeks had felt portentous. Our blackjack business, which required schlepping cash bankroll on carry-on luggage through airports, had been put on an indefinite hiatus. I had nothing to do.

I'd thought my character should shift. I'd thought my values ought to be refined. A demand had been made by the horror. And I would shift, I'd thought, and I would be refined, and I'd kept thinking it, and waiting.

The terror attacks didn't do it. And now with Burt's call the news cycle was shifting again. I muster the idea that the urgency, if any, of life belongs not to life but to ourselves.

He raised a significant eyebrow and nodded at me, sighing.

"We're bombing Afghanistan," Clem said.

I hadn't seen that coming. It was Sunday and we were stoned.

Take the Wheel

Piper Kerman

Do you want to drive?"

This question snapped my young self to attention, as I tore my eyes away from the open pastures, grown high with grass and wildflowers, that were starting to disappear in the summer dusk. I looked at my uncle, the tallest and gangliest of my mother's brothers, who had asked the question. We were alone in his car together, him in the driver's seat, me on the passenger side. We were bumping down Shaw's Road, an unlit country lane that would soon turn to gravel as it led down to the little New England cove where generations of our family have gathered every summer. It was dark enough that he had switched on the headlights, and the beams bounced in front of us, scaring off adolescent rabbits.

"What?" I wasn't sure if I had heard right.

"Do you want to drive the car?" I had never been behind the wheel of a car, was at least a year off from even being eligible for my learner's permit. It would never have occurred to me to ask to learn the so-familiar yet mysterious workings of a vehicle, the clear purview of adulthood which seemed so distant. Fourteen-year-olds didn't drive; it was against the rules. But suddenly I wanted nothing more than to do just that.

My mother's younger brothers loved cars, a love perhaps inherited from my grandmother, who still spoke wistfully about a blue convertible she'd owned decades before. I couldn't believe that my uncle, closer in age to me than to my mother, would let me drive his, and I couldn't imagine this would be okay with my parents. In the dim light I looked across the front seat at him, waiting for the offer to be rescinded. "Yes," I finally said.

He pulled over to the side of the road and put the car in park, still running. He got out and walked around the car, opened my door for me. I jumped out and ran through the headlight beams to hop into the driver's seat. I could see the shape of a stone farmhouse distant in the rearview mirror. The Volvo's tape player was on, probably the Police or Elvis Costello, as I stretched my feet toward the unfamiliar pedals on the floorboard. I really had no idea what I was doing.

With coaching from my uncle, I nervously pressed my foot on the gas and turned us back onto the blacktop. There wasn't another car, nor another person, in sight. Just me, a small teenage girl trying to control what suddenly seemed like an enormous car, and my now visibly nervous uncle, swerving down that country road. If I started to run us off into the fields, he would grab the wheel and steer us straight. Somehow I made a spectacularly wide right turn to get to the gravel that sloped down toward the cottage lights that edged the cove.

Ten minutes earlier I had been a little kid, a passenger in a grown-up's car, but now I was something altogether different. In those glorious, gleeful moments when I urged that powerful engine forward, I also set out toward becoming a grown woman, directing my own fate, for better or for worse. When we had almost reached the cove, my uncle told me to pull over, and we switched places, back to where we had started. "Don't tell your mother," he said with a grin, as he switched off the ignition.

Black Like Me

Haylee Harrell

It was recess, only halfway through the day, and a fight was already in progress. I can't recall what it was about. All I remember is the heat of a Utah summer afternoon and the separation of the two groups of fifth-grade girls on opposite sides of the large green field. I was stationed with my best friend and three or four other girls. My friend was in a fight with a girl who had bright crimson hair, who was on the far end of the field. There was a quiet brunette girl who was forced into being the messenger between the two groups. The recess period seemed as if it was lasting forever.

I wanted to go play four square but I couldn't leave my best friend's side. I was lying on my back and staring at the sky, which was so clear—light blue with only sparse clouds. I was so lost within my surroundings that I didn't even notice when the quiet messenger came rushing back to our group. When I sat up to look at her I noticed immediately how awkward she seemed. My best friend was prompting her to relay the message, but the shy girl just kept shaking her head. She looked down at the dark green grass and muttered, "It's not about you." My best friend perked up and stepped forward. "Who is it about then?" The messenger's eyes lifted for only a brief second, but it was long enough to focus her gaze on me. My best friend proclaimed, "If the message is about Haylee, then you have to tell me, because we're best friends and she would tell me anyways later." The messenger sighed and the air became thick. After a few seconds she stepped forward and whispered, "she said, 'I hate Haylee because she is black and I hate black people.'"

My stomach dropped. She hated me? Just because of my skin? I couldn't comprehend it. I always told everyone I was both Black and Italian, half and half. Yet this girl declared that she hated all of me because of half my ethnicity. My body sank to the ground and I became increasingly aware of all the eyes upon me. I was crying. The recess monitor was called over. Commotion ensued, though all I can recall clearly is my confusion. How could someone hate me just because I didn't look like them? I liked the same things as her, I did just as well in school, we shared the same friends, I talked like her. Our only difference was my skin, and she decided to hate me because of it. I knew that my skin was darker then everyone else's, but my mom's skin was white like theirs, so part of me was just like them. For the rest of elementary and middle school I tried to act just like everyone else so they couldn't find an excuse to hate me.

Eight years later, I have just barely accepted my full ethnicity and gained appreciation for both my cultures. But every now and then I recall that afternoon, and no matter where I am in my life, strong emotions of hate, fear, embarrassment, resentment, and sadness still arise.

The Night My Mother Refused to Cook Dinner

Michael Castleman

It must have been around 1960. I was ten years old and hungry, waiting impatiently for dinner. But my mother wasn't cooking. She wasn't even in the kitchen. She was in the living room reading Leon Uris's new novel, *Exodus*, about the SS *Exodus*, a ship full of concentration camp survivors that tried to dock in Palestine in 1947, but was turned away by the British authorities.

I whined about dinner. When are we going to eat? After I finish my book, my mother said. *Exodus* was a hot bestseller and she'd waited months to get it from the library. I knew my mother was an avid reader, but this was the first time my life had ever been disrupted by her devotion to the printed word. I didn't care how long she'd waited for the book or how much she anticipated reading it. I was hungry and demanded dinner. Tough luck, wait till I'm finished. *And the more you bother me, the longer it's going to take.*

Eventually, she finished, closed the book, and got a late dinner on the table amid grumbling from my father, my three brothers, and me.

It was a fleeting moment, but it stuck with me. My mother was totally devoted to our family. She served dinner like clockwork every evening, and nothing had ever changed her routine—until that book.

As a fourth- or fifth-grader, I'd read quite a bit for school and written book reports. Like a lot of my peers, I viewed the enterprise as a chore, something I had to endure before I could play. But a book had been so important to my mother that she'd blown off what I considered her most sacred duty. That could mean only one thing: Books were powerful, magical. That delayed dinner changed my relationship to reading. I realized that books could be so engrossing that nothing else mattered. That was the moment I took my first step toward becoming a writer.

Horns

Shalom Auslander

When I was a child, my mother told me that everyone in the world hated me. They hated me, she said, because I was a Jew.

So? I asked.

So nothing, she replied. So they hate you.

Not just the people on our street, who were "classic Jew-haters"; not just everyone in the town nearby, who were "card-carrying anti-Semites"; not just everyone in the world now, but everyone who'd ever lived, ever: Egyptians, Greeks, Romans, Spaniards, Italians, Germans, Christians, Catholics, Muslims.

I was sure she was wrong. I was sure they just hated her, which I could very well understand. She told me this when I was six, when I was thirteen, when I was fifteen and when I was seventeen. At eighteen, I went on a trip through Europe with some observant Orthodox friends; it was something of a symbolic trip, because we were at the age when we were getting ready to leave home, to head out into that strange new world outside the narrow religious one in which we had been raised. I was determined to find a new home for myself, something broader, more enlightened, less paranoid, less terrified.

One morning, we were on a Eurail train, headed, I believe, for Paris, when we decided to pray. We had on our yarmulkes, tzitzis, phylacteries, the whole outfit. A US Marine, in full camouflage, was seated in front of us, and he kept turning around, looking at us and smiling warmly. When we finished praying, he turned around again, and, in a heavy Southern accent, with absolutely no malice or hatred whatsoever—in fact, with an almost endearing, childlike curiosity—asked me if I wouldn't mind too terribly showing him my "Jew horns."

Not, he added, if it's like a big deal or something.

My first thought was that he was kidding.

My second thought was that he was serious.

My third thought was, Oh, shit—Mom was right.

If he had just called me a dirty Jew, it would have been okay. If he had just held me down and carved a swastika on my head—no biggie, I'll wear hats. But he went all the way to *horns*—to the Middle Ages, Christ-killing, money-lending, shape-shifting shit.

That was going to be a problem.

Not because of anti-Semitism. I could probably make it in a world fouled with ignorance. I could probably get by on a planet poisoned with petty prejudice and institutionalized hatred. But a world where my mother was right?

That was going to be a problem.

What Would Roland Do?

Benjamin Percy

Thirteen is the worst year of anybody's life, but I had an especially awful run. In trouble for fighting. In trouble for vandalism. In trouble for stealing. In trouble for grades. I remember my mother crying and running upstairs when I was suspended. I recall my father ripping up my report card and hurling the pieces across the room like the saddest sort of confetti, not saying a word, just staring at me with hooded eyes. They made the decision to pull me out, to put me in a different school with smaller classes and rougher discipline.

It was then that I first read Stephen King's *The Gunslinger*. Of course the plot grabbed me by my throat (which was pretty scrawny back then), but Roland was the real reason the book affected me so profoundly. Roland of Gilead, the lead character, the titular gunslinger. This might seem ridiculous to some people—but remember that I was thirteen at the time, leaving one school and joining another forty miles away. I can remember my parents telling me that the new school would change me—that change was good, I needed to change—and I agreed with them. I felt like a pitiful smear of human waste and was actively thinking to myself, *who do I want to be?*

Roland answered that question. He seemed the ultimate man. He lived by a knight's code of honor. He withstood pain with gritted teeth. He was disciplined, knowledgeable, strong. He was in the pursuit of something important—his presence in the world mattered. He was never the one to start a fight, but always the one left standing. He rarely spoke, but when he did, his words were wise and impactful. Silence, I came to understand, was knowing when to shut up. I became deeply reticent that summer—and the silence lasted until I graduated from high school.

Some might have mistaken it for being shy, but it was something else: I was a strategist, holding back, judging every word, every action, trying to decide its merit. You see those kids with the WWJD wristbands? I should have had a special one made—*What would Roland do?* I understand that this sounds horribly corny, but it's true, and back then it mattered to me more than anything in the world. My grades sharpened. I became painfully serious, my face absent of expression. Sometimes I would lie in bed and chide myself for something I had said or done that seemed to me ill-becoming, and it was as though, in the shadows shifting on my ceiling, the shape of the Gunslinger was taking form.

Since that long-ago summer, I've read *The Gunslinger* more than any other book (*Jesus' Son* by Denis Johnson and *Blood Meridian* by Cormac McCarthy take a close second and third). I'm still that little boy when I crack it open. But I'm a writer, too, and I especially love the hybrid quality of the narrative—it's a western, it's a fantasy, it's a horror novel, and it brings to mind legends of knights rattling their swords in battle, following a chivalrous code.

My father (with some help from me, though a teenager isn't worth much with a hammer) built the house we lived in then, in the nowhereland of sage flats and alfalfa fields that stretch between Bend and Redmond, Oregon. But after I left for college, they sold it and lit out for Portland. So when I go home to see them, I never feel as if I'm actually going home. I have returned to central Oregon several times, and each time, I drive past the old house and feel a blend of nostalgia . . . and gratitude that I'm no longer that skinny-armed punk toting a BB gun and a bad attitude.

Over the past year, I've been getting strange calls on my cell phone. "Roland?" a voice will say, "Is Roland there?" And I will say, "Sorry. Wrong number." But the other day, when my phone rang and I heard "Roland? Is this Roland?" I paused for a moment, debating whether to say *yes*.

"SILENCE, I CAME TO UNDERSTAND,

WAS KNOWING WHEN TO SHUT

UP. I BECAME DEEPLY RETICENT

THAT SUMMER—AND THE SILENCE

LASTED UNTIL I GRADUATED FROM

HIGH SCHOOL."

Fearless Flyer

Ashley Van Buren

sat in the window seat of the airplane on the eve of my twenty-fifth birthday, clutching a pill bottle and waiting for death to take over. A feeling of impending doom left me paralyzed with fear or sent me into a full-blown panic attack whenever I set foot in a small, confined space.

I was twelve years old when I got stuck in a crowded elevator at New York's Columbia Hospital. People screamed as the elevator dropped several floors, and with it went my confidence in any machinery that propelled humans off the ground. Years of biofeedback, some therapy sessions, and practice taking elevators one-floor-at-a-time followed.

Now on the plane we were taxiing to the runway for takeoff. The terrible sensation should have hit me by now. I was waiting for it, anticipating six long hours thinking about how the plane was going to crash and how I would die. How we would all die. But something was off this time. The fear and anxiety that kept me from taking jobs, taking risks, taking chances, *living life* didn't grip me as it had for the past thirteen years.

There was something else different about this particular trip: a pill no larger than a tiny pearl that my doctor had prescribed. I hated taking pills, but a lifetime lived in fear was a much worse prospect. This tiny pill jump-started my rational thinking. The chemicals helped my brain to release a confidant thought, a truth: *The plane will fly and you will arrive safely on the other side of the country. You will be okay.* Reason had finally won out over doom. In that moment, sitting on my Jet Blue flight from JFK to LAX, I was filled with calm. No anxiety. No fear. The plane sped down the runway, the wheels lifted up, and we began our ascent.

Hobo Beginnings

Dale Maharidge

This photograph was taken on our sixth day of riding as hobos on freight trains up and down the West Coast in April 1982. Photographer Michael S. Williamson and I, working at the *Sacramento Bee* newspaper, were assigned to find out about the newly unemployed living a redux of the 1930s. So we hopped on freight trains with them. Michael was twenty-five and I was twenty-six.

This began our thirty years of working together as a team documenting America—the struggle of workers and others left outside the system. Along the way, we won a Pulitzer Prize for one of our books, another book inspired Bruce Springsteen to write two songs, and we've recently coauthored our sixth book, *Someplace Like America: Tales from the New Great Depression.*

None of this would have happened if we'd not hit the rails in 1982. That hobo trip dictated the course of the rest of our professional lives. We feel our job description has been to document the other America, the one seen from a boxcar door—the backside of

a country in denial about the majority of its people dwelling in the shadows. Was it chance that we ended up on that train, or are some things destined? I tend to believe the latter.

I look angry in the picture because Michael had to leap across to another grain car to set up the camera on a timer—then jump back. The train was going some seventy miles an hour. One slip, he would have been ground beneath the wheels. I barked at him that it was not worth the risk. I can say this now because he did not perish: it was worth it. This picture, more than any other taken since, defines who we are.

Adopting My Son

Christoph Marshall

At twenty, I told my parents that I was gay. My mom suggested I move to another city—to help her avoid the shame I would bring upon her and the family. My dad told me I would lead an unhappy, lonely life because I would never have a family. With my boyfriend's support, it was easy enough to dismiss what my mom had said. But my dad's words really frightened me.

Four years later, I moved to New York City to attend graduate school. When I learned of the Big Brothers of New York City program I joined immediately. I then got the opportunity to mentor two kids, but eventually their parents blocked access and later moved without leaving word of their new address. I felt a keen sense of frustration and a strong need not to allow such a situation to repeat itself.

At the time some of my coupled gay friends were talking about adopting kids or having babies with lesbian friends. So there *was* a gay life that treasured family. I decided to give it a shot on my own, educating myself how best to file an application and look for an agency. Several agencies were helpful, but none could really help, for one reason or another.

Every agency that receives funding from the city is required to write a home study for prospective adoptive parents, regardless of whether or not they consider the applicant suitable for the children in their custody. So I went to the Catholic Archdiocese and asked for a home study. I was told in no uncertain terms that my home would not be considered for any child in their custody—for which I was prepared. Nonetheless, I insisted that they still write the home study I requested. It took nearly a year before a social worker first interviewed me, then came to my apartment, and ultimately wrote a report about me, my abilities to raise a child, and my home.

With the Catholic home study in hand, I applied for ten kids from the Blue Book, a catalog of kids freed for adoption. Each one was from a different agency, not on ADHD medication, and all in the age range from eight to twelve. I reckoned these children were probably stable and old enough to go to school independently; while they were in school I imagined I'd have enough time to do my graduate work.

With one exception, every agency wrote back declining my application without further consideration, some with particularly offensive language. St. Christopher Ottilie, one of the larger Catholic agencies in the city, however, had Eddie, and was willing to introduce us. Eddie was described as a high-performing, intelligent thirteen-year-old Hispanic child. I met the social worker, who was evidently very close with Eddie, and we set up an appointment. Eddie and I first met at the agency's office in Forest Hills, Queens, and I immediately connected with him over an introductory walk. He was incredibly good-natured, well spoken, and well behaved; I immediately felt a connection, and also felt that I would be up to the challenge. We each separately told his social worker that the meeting had been a success. A week or so later, I picked Eddie up at the home where he was living, and again we went for a walk. This time, he seemed depressed, and conversation with him was superficial and slow going.

Still, I felt good about Eddie, and wanted to push forward. But after the second meeting, I received a phone call from his social worker that Eddie had decided to go live with another family. No explanation was given, other than that it seemed the people he was living with had urged him to choose another family.

I was so disappointed that I could hardly find the motivation to pursue my efforts to find a child. Yet the wheels were turning, and eventually another child turned up, and I went to visit him in a home in Westchester. Again, I liked this child very much, and hoped I would be able to make the decision to adopt him. But he was difficult. He had a history of running away from home, his performance in school was abysmal, and he seemed simultaneously to crave and shun the idea of joining me in my quest to build a family. In the end, after several meetings, and months of back and forth, I decided I was not up to the task.

Shortly thereafter, I received another call from Eddie's social worker asking whether I was still interested in adopting Eddie. Since I had seen him last, almost a year ago, he had moved in with another family, but the situation wasn't working out. Eddie had reconsidered, and wanted to come and live with me after all. Without hesitation, I arranged to meet with his social worker the same day, and arrangements were made for Eddie to come visit again. This time he was the same Eddie I remembered from our first meeting.

After a full afternoon of walking around in the city, and getting to know each other somewhat better, it became clear that the reason he initially chose not to live with me was that his then–foster parents advised heavily against living with a single—probably gay—white guy who would never be able to understand his cultural heritage. But now, that family was rejecting *him* because of cultural conflicts and the belief he was gay—which, it turned out, he was.

I was able to foresee many problems that could and would arise from a gay child moving in with me, but it was also clear that, in addition to an intellectually stimulating environment, I had something very valuable to provide him: comfort with his sexuality, a rare commodity in the early nineties, even in New York City. I instantly realized that this was the challenge I was looking for, and decided—on the subway, on our way to my place—that I was up for it. I hoped he was too.

Adopting My Dad

Eddie Comacho

Christoph and I were on the subway, headed to his graduate student housing on the Upper East Side. Although I had already met with him several times, I had never been to his place before.

I was different from other teens. All I really wanted was to be part of a family. In foster care since the age of seven, my previous experiences with foster parents were all emotionally draining. There was always an expectation. You were there not to be yourself, but to fill the shoes they had already designed for you. Most prospective adoptive parents were not comfortable with the topic of homosexuality; their suspicions that I might be gay inevitably turned out to be a deal breaker.

And now I was in unchartered territory.

I had heard that Christoph was probably gay too. With him, I felt that I could finally be myself. As I sat on that train, my mind was racing miles a minute. Christoph seemed very open. I felt as if I could tell him anything, no matter how weird. But I was still terrified to be completely honest, recalling others' reactions. My mouth got really dry as I tried to muster the courage to tell him that I was gay, while preparing myself for the worst—again. The train was just about to pull into the 51st Street station when I blurted, "By the way, I think you should know that I am gay."

Christoph looked completely surprised. I could see him choosing his next words carefully. "Well that's fine. So, how long have you known?" Then an awkward silence and I felt the old guilt pangs. And then he said, "You're fine. We should talk about it a little bit more, but let's not miss our transfer."

As we got off the train and started to walk toward the escalators I felt as if I was floating. He seemed completely cool with it. It was at that moment that I decided I wanted to be adopted by Christoph. I was fourteen years old.

Running

Mira Ptacin

hadn't planned on getting pregnant: I was taking the pill, and never missed a day. Still, it happened. (I'm that .01 percent.) It wasn't easy but I embraced it. And even though we had only been dating for three months, Andrew and I got engaged, agreeing on three things we knew for sure: that we loved each other very much, that our baby was made from this love, and that we were going to do our best to nourish the new life we had created.

Five months later, we went to an appointment that would reveal the sex of our baby. During the ultrasound the doctors revealed three things we couldn't have known: that the baby was a girl, that she was terminally ill, and that she had no chance of survival outside my womb.

She died a few weeks later. A month after that, Andrew and I got married. Life went on. We tried to move on too. We got into routines. We had dinner parties. Andrew had been training for the New York Marathon, and invited me on his shorter runs, but I declined my husband's invitations. My body felt as if it was filled with cement, yet fragile and faulty. My heart was electric and popping with rage.

I desperately sought quick-fix solutions to suppress the feelings I didn't want to have. I tried denial—denial of the magnitude of what had just happened. I cut off my relationships and embraced solitude. For weeks, I spent my life zoned out on a couch with a tub of peanut butter ice cream, flipping through TV channels. I couldn't read, I couldn't write, I didn't even want to leave the house. So I'd sit and wait: wait for my husband to come home from work, wait for the day to end, wait to feel better again. But the longer I avoided examining my grief, the stronger it got.

I looked for someone to blame. When Andrew kissed me, let alone touched my shoulder, I'd tense up, sometimes even get livid. Sometimes the hardness in my heart would melt, and I'd cry and apologize to him for my vehemence and seclusion. Revealing my own tenderness felt like defeat, but the balm of compliance soothed my pain. I'd beg Andrew to give me a solution to ease my sorrow. But he couldn't. No one could.

I saw a therapist, who eventually diagnosed me as clinically depressed with PTSD. She strongly recommended that I be medicated, and, with her pen, scribbled the name of an (expensive) Upper West East Side psychiatrist onto a piece of paper and sent me on my way.

I am clinically depressed. Once I said the words out loud, I felt as if I'd opened the festered secrecy of my heart. PTSD. I continued to confess rapidly and urgently, ready to accept the previously unforeseen liberation. But medication?

I had never wanted to be a person who popped a "happy pill"—it was too New York, too cliché. I simply wanted to end my suffering. Yet, as sure as I was about my longing for serenity, I was ambivalent about going on antidepressants. What if they didn't work? What if the pills didn't make me content but diluted my grief instead?

A day before my intake appointment with the psychiatrist, I received a call from a close friend back in Maine. He'd been concerned about me, and called once a week to check in. When I told him that I'd found a solution to my misery and explained it, my friend scoffed at my enthusiasm.

"You fool," he teased. "You ain't no Girl, Interrupted. Why don't you just go for a jog instead?"

And in that instant, everything changed.

In the beginning, I couldn't run a single mile. I'd start off strong, following Andrew's pace, get a side-stitch then quit. I'd fault Andrew for going too fast, too slow, for talking too much, for being too quiet. But he wouldn't give up on me that easily, or let me do the same. Soon, we compromised on a rhythm—he'd move a little slower, I'd push a little harder. I got up to three miles, then five. I stopped following Andrew's rhythm and focused on my own: my breath, my stride, my pace. I stopped being so afraid of feeling pain. Really, I stopped being afraid of feeling things.

I never ended up going on antidepressants. Instead, I run. I'm training for the Chicago Marathon, and I'm up to eighteen miles. Every time my foot hits the ground and I pick the other one up, I'm reminded that running—the art of literally putting one foot in front of the other—brought me back to life.

At First Sight

L. Nichols

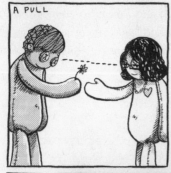

Piazza San Marco

Julian Voloj

The photo was taken in 2002 at San Marco Square in Venice. Lisa and I had met briefly before in New York City. She was twenty-six, hailed from the Midwest, and living in Brooklyn. I was twenty-eight, born in Germany to Colombian parents, and living in Brussels. She came to visit me in Europe for our first "real" date.

When we kissed for the first time, we both knew that this was it. Everyone thought we were crazy, but against all odds, everything worked out. A year later I moved to New York. We got married the following year, and today we are happy parents of two boys.

I took this photo with a self-timer.

First Kiss

Scott Muska

It happened on a fall afternoon in 1999, the year Clinton was acquitted in the Monica Lewinsky affair and Ricky Martin was campaigning for possession of every woman's heart in America and maybe the world.

I'd been gearing up for it all day. I was nervous, and extremely so; you wouldn't believe how nervous I was, actually, unless you were once a twelve-year-old boy who was about to kiss a girl of no familial relation for the first time.

Notes had been exchanged. In a rare written moment of confidence and bravado, I had broached the subject in a note to Brittnee—the apple of my sixth-grade eye—that I had composed during second period social studies class. We'd been given a few minutes of free time to get started on our homework, but I wrote instead. I wrote to her that I liked her so much I wanted to kiss her. It was one of those impulsive things a guy sometimes does just to see if he can actually make something happen. I gave it to a friend who said he'd pass it to Brittnee in the class they had together the next period, and then I walked around anxiously until the end of lunch, when she slipped me a response.

It was on. She liked me, and wanted to kiss me too. So we would kiss. That day, in fact. She said we could do it after school, on the sidewalk where we said our good-byes before she walked to her sister's car and I got on the bus.

I can't be 100 percent sure, but I'm fairly certain the moment after I read this note was the first instance in my life I ever executed a sweeping fist-pump.

At the end of the day, we exited our middle school building and clasped our hands together to make them look like a single person's two hands in a prayer formation (the more intimate method of hand-holding), and began walking. I remember how sweaty my hand was. My hands are constantly sweaty, but that day was even worse. She was calm, though, and that helped.

We reached the spot a few steps from my bus where we would part hands and ways on a daily basis, and we faced each other. Neither of us said anything. I giggled a little bit, like an idiot, and she just looked up at me and stood up on her tiptoes. I bent down slightly, our lips met for a second, and it was the greatest I think I'd ever felt in my entire life leading up to that moment. I pulled—no, drifted, I was floating—away, thinking a peck was exactly what a guy gets for his first kiss, and that maybe I'd give the whole making-out thing my brother was always talking about a try in another three years or so.

But Brittnee had a different idea. She brought her lips back to mine, and we kissed again for at least five seconds. I could have lived in those five seconds for the next five years. I remember tasting her Dr. Pepper-flavored Lip Smackers balm, and wanting to open my eyes just a little bit to see how beautiful a girl could be up close (of course I didn't, because I knew a thing or two about kissing etiquette). There was no tongue involved, just two adolescents touching lips and moving them around a little bit. It was amazing, and I almost fainted when we parted and I walked toward the bus, where I would sit for the next twenty minutes smiling like an idiot while I tried to explain what had just happened to my best friend, Evan.

I can say it without any doubt: That was the moment that changed everything. I didn't become a different person, really, but something inside me was altered irrevocably. Kissing a girl was awesome, really, and it immediately became the most important thing in my life. It was a simple thing, really, one person's lips touching someone else's, but at the same time it wasn't.

Waited thirty-two years for first kiss.
— *Kristi King*

First kiss. During church. Sorry, Jesus.
— *Jordan H.*

My first kiss was her sister.
— *Joseph P. Molinari*

First kiss . . . on stage. Biggest fear.
— *Lisa Burnett*

Scared of girls, until first kiss.
— *Mark Rosenblum*

Redefined "best friends"
with first kiss.
— *Jen J.*

First dances lead to first kisses.
— *Kayla S.*

First kiss bad. Practice made perfect.
— *Junior K.*

The Crüe

Sara Lovelace

Tiffani smelled like cigarette smoke and perm. She lived in a trailer. Good manners forced me to accept an invitation to her slumber party, and I was the only girl who showed up that night. Tiffani spent the first few hours crying and calling the other girls from school "tramps" and "cunts" for not coming. She told me that *Hee Haw,* her favorite show, was coming on that night. I'd never seen *Hee Haw* or eaten Star Crunch snack cakes or heard the word "cunt" before. Those things were exotic to me. I began to like Tiffani that night. I also hated that I liked Tiffani because this would cause problems at school. I knew that it was Tiffani or everyone else, and I would have to choose.

Her brother, Dustin, came into the trailer with a can of beer and a cigarette. When he saw it was a party of two he cursed mean kids, girls, teachers, bosses, pretty much everything and everyone. His sister's sad slumber party was more proof to him that the world was a cruel place. He waved a five-dollar bill in front of us and said he was taking us to the gas station for as much candy as we wanted.

In his Camaro, Dustin rolled down the windows and turned the volume on the tape deck all the way up. "This is my fucking song," he said. It was Mötley Crüe's "Smokin' in the Boys Room," a band and a song I'd never heard. I wouldn't describe myself as sheltered at that age. Filtered, maybe. Too much Montessori and Peter, Paul and Mary and *Free to Be You and Me*. All good stuff, but it left me highly vulnerable to the likes of Mötley Crüe. I had a hankering for the unfamiliar. My parents hoped that it would lead to a fine study abroad program during my college years. It didn't.

I somehow sensed, at that moment, that I belonged in a Camaro blaring the Crüe, that cotillions were not a part of my future. It may have happened even if I hadn't gone to Tiffani's that night, but I doubt it. Being the only girl who showed up at that party gave me a feeling of solidarity with Tiffani. We were outsiders, though she was one by birth, I by choice.

The other girls knew that I had gone to Tiffani's, and at school on Monday they left the lunch table when I sat down beside them. I saw Tiffani coming toward me with her tray, and I wanted to ignore her but I couldn't. She sat down and pulled a Star Crunch snack cake from the front pocket of her flannel shirt. "I hate this shitty food," she said. "Want half?"

Uncaged

Alan Rabinowitz

As a child I had a very severe stutter. My stuttering defined everything about me. It was the kind of stutter where the air is blocked, so when I tried to say hard consonants my throat closed down. Unfortunately, one of the worst things for me to say was my own last name: *Rabinowitz*.

I'm not certain if I was thirteen or fourteen, but I do remember everything else about the one particular day that changed my life. In Far Rockaway, Queens, in the sixties we shopped at places where you would call in your order ahead of time, and the store would bag the groceries for you. My mom asked me to go pick up an order waiting behind the cash register under our name. I was in a total panic. I'd have to announce our name to retrieve the bags. If I managed to get through the "r" then the "b" would stop me—those hard consonants were misery.

After waiting anxiously in line, my turn came at the checkout counter. I went mute and pointed to the visible bunch of bags with my name on them. I tried to say my name, but, as feared, my throat started to block. In trying to break the block, my head jerked, as if I was having spasms. Still unable to get any sound out, I banged my hand on the counter, staring intently at those grocery bags. I could feel everyone's eyes on me.

The girl helping me was, of course, embarrassed. She turned away and said to the rest of the line, "Oh please excuse him, he's retarded." When you stutter you're always looking for a way out. So I started to act how I thought a retarded person would act, flailing my arms and legs wildly—sort of like Joe Cocker on stage. I then went behind the counter, grabbed the bags and ran out of the store. When I got out of sight I threw the bags to the ground. I was furious.

I had let the adult world judge me again and, worst of all, this time I had given in to their judgment. I wasn't angry with the girl at the counter or the other people in line; I hated myself. I felt like the lowest being on earth. If I had had a knife at that moment I would have stabbed myself. And then I said out loud: "I will never, ever, let people judge me again." The resolve took hold of me unlike anything I had ever felt. I calmly gathered all the groceries and went home.

I had always wanted to be like everybody else, to be equal with them, to be *normal*. Now none of that was good enough. I decided I would be *better* than everyone else. I would do more than anyone thought I could do. From that moment on, I was determined not to live by other people's rules. I would excel far beyond the norm in everything I did. I remember that day, that moment, more vividly than any other from my childhood; it has defined my life ever since.

But sheer determination didn't make life easier, and my stuttering didn't improve. Frustrated with trying to live up to others' perceptions or expectations of me, I just stopped trying to communicate with people. I turned to the only living things I could speak to without stuttering: my little New York City–style pets. Each day after school, I would gather up my hamster, my green turtle, or my chameleon, and retreat into a corner of my bedroom closet. In the darkness I didn't have to face myself. Instead I would talk to my animals and pour my heart out.

My father recognized my love for animals at an early age. Though he never fully understood my dependence on them, he realized they reached me in ways that he could not. If I had a particularly bad week at school, my dad would take me to the Big Cat House at the Bronx Zoo. There I would stand in front of each of the animal's cages, soaking up their strength and power. Pacing back and forth, these huge beautiful beasts were locked within the four barred walls of their cages, with no way to tell the human world what they felt, how they were being treated, or what they truly wanted. I felt a deep bond. Their physical cage represented my locked mind, powerful and stuck. And the cat was me. It was the one place in the world, besides my closet, where I felt comfortable.

Just as I talked to my animals in my closet, I would get up close to the cages and talk to the tigers and the jaguar. "I will find a place for us," I said.

Years later, I remembered my promise. I became a zoologist because I knew I needed the mechanisms, the tools, and the credibility to keep my promise to animals, particularly the cats. I loved being in the jungle, away from human beings, where I didn't have to speak. In the more than three decades of my career, I have never lost that feeling of "rightness" when I am in the wildest places of the world. Even now, with a wife and family, I'm still trying to find my comfort zone between the animal world and the human world. I strive to give the animals a voice before theirs and mine are lost forever.

To the Rescue

Ellen Sussman

I was shooting hoops with my brother in the backyard when I heard the screams. I stopped mid-dribble and looked at the upstairs window of my house. My brother slapped the ball out of my hands.

"Hey," I said. "Something's going on."

"It's just Mom and Renee fighting for a change."

Mitch and I were nine and eight; our big sister, Renee, was nineteen. I could hear her sobbing through the open window.

"But I love the dress," she wailed.

I tore into the house and ran up the stairs, taking them two at a time. I had always been scared of the fights between my sister and my mother. My mother was fun and loving with Mitch and me; she was tyrannical with my sister. Renee was our half sister, my dad's daughter from an earlier marriage. Was that the reason? Or was it a personality clash? My mother was big and bold; my sister, shy and unassuming. The fights were always the same: My mother yelled and my sister cried. My mother bullied and my sister obeyed.

"It's hideous," my mother shouted. They were standing in my parents' bedroom, in front of the large mirror that hung over the bureau.

Both the mirror frame and the bureau were painted with flowers. I remember the day a man came to our house and painted flowers on all the furniture in my parents' bedroom and I thought: *When I grow up, I want that.*

My sister was wearing a pink gown, floor length and satiny. I was a tomboy, and I thought it was ugly.

"You don't wear a big bow on your chest when you have a big bust," my mother spat. "Everyone knows that."

"I want it," my sister whined.

"Take it back," my mother ordered. "You're not wearing that ugly thing to Rosie's wedding."

"It's beautiful," I said, and even now, so many years later, I remember a kind of silence that hung in the room for a moment. Had I ever defended my sister before? Had I ever challenged my mother's authority?

"What are you doing here?" my mother asked.

"You should keep it," I told my sister.

My sister stared at me, her eyes swollen, her mouth hanging open.

"It's hideous—" my mother started to say.

"No, it isn't. And she can wear it if she wants to. She can wear anything she wants."

The moment blurs in my memory after that. I don't even remember if Renee kept the dress and wore it, big bow prominently displayed. But I do remember a startling sensation as I stood in the doorway. I felt big. I felt superhero strong. I tucked that new power deep inside of me and walked away.

The Shed

Colin Nissan

Behind our house was a shed. Not just any shed, a magic shed. Growing up, whenever I wanted to buy anything—a new shirt, an action figure, a bike—I got the same response from my father.

"I have one in the shed," he'd say with great certainty, gazing off as if mentally locating its exact position inside.

The disturbing part about this wasn't just that he was keeping me from getting new things, but that he was right. Somehow, inevitably there would be one in the shed. An old, broken, spiderweb-entombed one, but one nonetheless. And for that reason, I couldn't argue with him. I could plead, but I couldn't argue.

I learned not to ask for much as a kid. It was generally better to go without than to go with something from the shed. Even the mere mention that one of us may be "in the market" for an item sent his wheels spinning. Colors, sizes, styles—he had exactly what we were looking for.

The shed's contents were the culmination of years of Saturday morning garage sales—suburban treasure hunts chasing hand-drawn arrows all over Concord, Massachusetts, stuffing our car with other people's junk. Chipped wine glasses, obsolete audio equipment, old board games with missing pieces. Anything that my father deemed valuable, which was often things simply made from a material he deemed valuable. Like metal. As if he had plans to melt it down and cast it into something grander.

Growing up in Concord, I had no reason to feel we were poor. We weren't rich by any means, but we were perfectly fine. Every so often, the lines became blurred because, in comparison, many in Concord were loaded. I'd be reminded of this periodically as the breezes from a passing Mercedes-Benz or BMW sent the duct tape on one of our beaters fluttering.

My father grew up poor among a small population of Iraqi Jews in Baghdad, and he proudly brought his instinctive Middle Eastern–bazaar mentality to the unprepared bluebloods of Concord. Every transaction involved a haggling process—a series of exchanges that made my ten-year-old toes curl in embarrassment.

"But sir, surely your asking price is negotiable given the glaring absence of not one but two forks in this lovely fondue set."

Each negotiation ended the same way—twenty-five cents off a one-dollar piece of garbage, a bewildered Concordian, and a triumphant smile on my father's face.

I could see that smile beaming in the rearview mirror all the way home, as I sat perilously wedged between purchases in the back seat. "What fools they are to part with such treasures . . . and at such a price." When I think of the times I saw my father truly happy, these rank highly.

The funny thing is, in the earlier years of these crap-gathering missions, I was convinced he was a savvy shopper with an eye for the truly valuable, like a buyer from Sotheby's dispatched to the suburbs in search of heirlooms. He spoke about the things he bought with such reverence and sophistication that I had little reason to believe otherwise. Except, of course, for my mother's decidedly unenthusiastic reactions when we unloaded the car every weekend.

"Wouldn't this brass dolphin look elegant here?" he'd propose, placing it on the dining room table to show her.

While the occasional aquatic figurine made it inside, we loaded 90 percent of his booty straight into the shed. Getting things in there was never the problem. Getting things out, however, was. These were hazardous extractions. Expeditions. Digs that would have given Richard Leakey the sweats. To this day if I close my eyes, I can still feel the rusty chill from the metal latch on the door. I can still hear the foreboding creak as it opened. I can still smell the memories of a thousand strangers' attics wafting from within.

I remember going to my friends' houses and seeing their sheds with hammers hanging from peg boards and boxes carefully labeled and stacked. There was no stacking or cataloging for us. No entry procedure whatsoever for new arrivals. Things were thrown, crammed and squeezed in anywhere they could possibly fit, teetering on top of last weekend's purchases, waiting to get the call. Tires waiting for cars we didn't own, bow ties waiting for proms ten years in the future, Christmas ornaments waiting for us to convert.

My biggest recurring fear upon opening the door to the shed, which was situated in the dense woods behind our house, was that a crazed rodent would attach itself to my face, clawing my eyes out while I wrestled it to the ground. Judging by the bounty of mysterious nests, webs, cocoons and droppings the shed contained, my fear was far from unfounded. This was no longer my father's property; Mother Nature had claimed it for herself—as if she had assessed its contents and thought no one would mind.

One Saturday, we were preparing for a family trip and needed a couple of extra suitcases. My father, brother, and I went out back on a Suitcase Dig. "There are some leather beauties in the back," my father said. "Golden-brown."

After an hour or so of clearing the way, passing each other boxes like relief workers in an Oxfam air drop, we spotted something brown. Golden-brown, just as he said. A few more minutes of maneuvering and we had them. My brother pulled the biggest one out and carried it onto the back lawn.

That's when his face went white.

He placed the bag down and backed away from it as if he heard a ticking inside.

"What?" I said.

"It's . . . moving," he said.

"What do you mean, it's moving?" my father said, with utter disbelief that anything could have broken the seal of his hermetic storage.

The suitcase sat on the lawn for what seemed like an hour, the three of us circling it from a distance. Watching, listening, tossing pebbles and gently prodding it with long sticks.

And that's when I saw it.

A ripple underneath the mahogany leather. A pulse, a stretch, a wave. My father approached the bag, still refusing to believe anything could be wrong. He knelt carefully down beside it, placed his hand on the zipper and ripped it open.

Out of the bag emerged what can only be described as an ocean of mice. A tidal wave of hundreds of gray, frightened, light-deprived rodents stampeding toward us like bulls at high noon in Pamplona.

My worst fear had come true. The shed was, indeed, the house of horrors I always suspected it was. As the three of us ran for our lives, screaming like seven-year-olds, and I saw the genuine terror in my father's eyes, all I could think was, "Is this what you wanted? Are you happy now, you sick son-of-a-bitch?"

It was at this moment, as that herd of tiny pink feet steadily gained on me, when everything became clear. All the Saturdays, all the strange purchases and my father's adamant deflections of logic to defend them, came flooding back to me. Whatever glimmer I held on to that my father was a seasoned connoisseur of artifacts instantly vanished. This wasn't how everyone spent their Saturdays; this wasn't how everyone shopped.

Through these knickknacks, I think he felt he was getting a tiny piece of what all these rich families in Concord had. Sure, they might have huge houses and fancy cars, but when he knocked seventy-five cents off their half-melted candles, he won.

The shed, to him, was America. Opportunity. It could house all the things he never had growing up in Iraq and all the things he desperately felt we'd one day need. It was a tiny room filled with thousands of little victories, and my father could never throw out a victory.

Curtain Call

Attila Kalamar

In 1979 my aunt Eva, cousin Tibor, and I got permission to go on a two-week boat cruise on the Danube River that would take us out of Romania and through the Iron Curtain. Obtaining permission for such a trip during Ceausescu's reign was very difficult, especially for a seventeen-year-old.

We left my hometown of Miercurea-Ciuc in the middle of April, just as spring crawled up the Carpathian Mountains of Transylvania. After an eight-hour train and bus ride we boarded the boat at a river port in Turnu Magurele. The first leg of the trip included stops in Belgrade; Budapest; and Bratislava, Czechoslovakia, before leaving the Iron Curtain. On the fifth day the boat arrived in Vienna. We were scheduled to dock for two days.

We spent the first day going to various individual stores and shopping centers. I could not believe the difference in lifestyle on the other side of the Iron Curtain. At the time, I remember thinking that the people on this side had everything and we, on the other side, had hardly anything. On our side, we had to stand in line for flour and cooking oil. Whenever lines formed outside the small gray stores, we

> "When we got to the palace our group lined up to enter the building. I found myself last in line, and as we climbed the stairs, I noticed a bathroom just inside on the left. Swiftly, I walked in alone."

joined them, because no matter what they were selling we knew we needed it. I even had a tooth pulled without Novocain because the dentist couldn't get the drug.

I was overwhelmed by the abundance in Vienna. I saw a guy drive a car with a bicycle strapped on its back and I could not figure out why he bothered; it seemed like having a hang-glider on a back of an airplane. It didn't make any sense to me. After a long day, we returned to the boat. But, overstimulated, I had a hard time falling asleep that night. Something felt wrong. Did we deserve to live in relative poverty on the other side? Were these people better than us? I wanted to understand, but I couldn't.

The next morning we found out that some fellow passengers did not come back from the shopping excursion, instead they took the golden opportunity to escape. The captain of the boat collected our passports to discourage the rest of us from any similar ideas. After breakfast we got on a bus for a sightseeing trip to Schonbrunn Palace, located outside of Vienna. I still had a restless feeling inside me during the ride that I could not shake. The beauty surrounding me was powerless against this feeling. Something was wrong and needed to be corrected.

When we got to the palace our group lined up to enter the building. I found myself last in line, and as we climbed the stairs, I noticed a bathroom just inside on the left. Swiftly, I walked in alone. By the time I finished taking care of some personal business the entire tour group, including my aunt and cousin, were all out of sight.

This was *my* golden opportunity, the moment my life changed forever, the moment of my rebirth. I knew that once I left, there could be no turning back. This was a one-way ticket to a new life. With ten shillings in my pocket and the clothes on my back, I walked out of the palace and through the front garden. Then, I kept walking for hours to put some distance between me and my old life. When I stopped and the adrenaline wore off, it hit me. I was alone in a place I didn't know and I didn't speak German or English. All I knew was that I wanted to make it to America and at seventeen years old nothing was impossible.

Today, I live in America, and I have a bicycle on the back of my car. Life is good.

Photo Finish

Kimberly Rose

The proof was in a packet of photos I had just picked up from CVS. Getting back the cardboard envelopes, I remember the eagerness and excitement I felt to see my two-year-old daughter's beautiful face shining with joy as she blew out the candles, opened her presents, and ate her cake.

There were at least sixty photographs inside. Bubbie and Za-yde (Grandma and Grandpa in Yiddish), Isabella, Ariella, everyone was in them. Except me. I was only a sliver of a shoulder, a hand on a child's arm, fingers cutting a cake, a nose kissing a frosting-covered cheek. Never all of me. Not one single picture of just me, not even one of my daughter and me.

I kept shuffling through the stack, not believing this was it, but it was. It was as if to my husband, Jim, who took the photos, I did not exist. He didn't want to see me in his album of life. He could not see me and, unfortunately, I was disappearing, ghosting away until I was some sort of iconic mother-wife without a name.

It was not only the loss of love that hit me in that moment, it was the loss of self, realizing that what we had was not what I had thought. Talk about a wake-up call. Hey, your husband doesn't love you, he never did, he never will, he doesn't even *see* you.

My spirits sank and never got back up.

I remembered earlier moments like this. We were looking at our neighbor's honeymoon pictures from five years earlier and seeing the many, many pictures her husband had taken of her. One stuck out: She had a dewy, just-out-of-bed look, with so much love in her eyes as she gazed at her husband through the lens.

I was jealous. There was no such photo of me after seven years of marriage, and I knew, in that moment, that there never would be. My husband had no desire to capture me or my love on film.

Sitting outside CVS in my car, I realized what I had known since seeing those honeymoon photographs but had denied all these years: that if I wanted to be loved like that, I would have to leave the marriage.

After my divorce, one of the first things I did was hire a professional photographer to take beautiful pictures of me. I wasn't at my lowest weight, wasn't tan, and I didn't have time to find really great outfits, but that wasn't the point. I needed to have my own photo album, one that featured: me. I wanted proof, forever, that I existed.

I got them back today and can't stop looking at them. I feel as if my soul exploded and out came me, out from the slivers, the corners and the shadows, into the light.

True Calm

Laura Cathcart Robbins

When my two sons and I arrived at the party, it was in full-swing chaos. The ball pit was closed because someone had "sullied" it, but kids were piling in anyway. A woman holding an infant had been pushed into the "cake table" (she and the infant were fine—the cake, not so much). Children rifled through the goodie bags that were supposed to be "parting gifts." The balloon artist kept scaring children by accidentally popping his balloon animals.

I took in the entire scene with a mixture of pity and smugness. *I* would have never let things get so out of control.

I saw the hostess trying to piece the cake back together so the "Happy Birthday Louie" was legible. Just then, her husband entered the party. He had arrived from London and come straight from the airport. His face was stern as he sought her out with his eyes, semigraciously accepting greetings or handshakes as he combed the room for her.

I braced myself for the blow-up. Surely he would lay in to her now. What husband wouldn't? She saw him and rose to her feet, her hands covered in blue icing. Her eyes were pleading; his, still stern and resolute.

At that moment my smugness disappeared and I felt not pity, but compassion for her. I knew how it felt to fail and have your husband blame you for it. I knew it all too well. I wanted to rush between them and delay the inevitable—his harsh words, her tears.

I couldn't comprehend what happened next. She closed her eyes and leaned into him, resting her head on his shoulder. He held her tenderly; eyes closed as well and rocked her gently back and forth. The chaos around them disappeared. He was not her tormentor, but her comforter.

Tears sprang easily to my eyes. I was mesmerized by the power of the love I saw in front of me. He loved her enough be her place of solace in the midst of chaos. She trusted him enough to let him.

Until that moment, I didn't believe that kind of love was possible.

Wally and Beaver

Jeff Church

Investment and Reward," said my father in reference to the idea of raising two piglets for slaughter in the spring of 1981, the money-raising activity that my brother and I would carry out in the great state of Washington when he was eleven and I was ten. The three of us had been living in the north end of Tacoma, but when my father remarried, we uprooted and moved to a larger house that sat on four acres, thirty miles south in the rural confines of a podunk town called Puyallup with our new mother and sister. "You raise the piglets and sell them for meat when they reach four hundred pounds . . . turn thirty dollars into three hundred and fifty . . . investment and reward," said my father, who was quietly excited about the opportunities that one could have while living on substantial land.

Like all kids, we wanted stuff: video game consoles, BMX parts from overseas, signature skateboard decks from California, things we'd seen in magazines or advertised between Saturday cartoons like *Captain Caveman*. My father's upbringing was different from ours; he had grown up in the coastal town of Newport, Oregon, where my grandparents grew their own vegetables and the meat and shellfish was hunted, trapped, or fished-out by them personally. An activity such as, say, shooting, field-dressing, and quartering a black-tailed deer wasn't anything to get squeamish over. If you ate meat, an unavoidable first step was killing it.

My father wasn't the type to just hand out money for things his kids wanted. It would have been a disservice to give his kids stuff every time they had a wild thought. Instead, he wanted us to see how things were earned, learn the value of a dollar. What's more, the pace of earning that money would give you time to ponder if you truly wanted what you were saving for.

When we picked up the two piglets, they were cute. They had dog-like personalities. I can't remember whose idea it was to give them names but, in hindsight, it was a bad idea, because it swung the pendulum closer to pet and farther from a cold warehouse term such as "investment." We gave them the handles Wally and Beaver after the Emmy-nominated *Leave it to Beaver*—a program that not only provided us with quality yuks, but also delivered baked-in moral lessons for all to pack out by show's end. That summer, my brother and I proceeded with the tasks of handling our investment. We fed and watered the pigs daily, cleaned their pens when they needed it, fed them apples as treats. And as their caretakers, the pigs were happy to see us. They would do circles when you gave them fresh hay to bed down on, and they showed us appreciation in the same way a dog would.

Yet six months later the day came when we were to turn the pigs into product. I was at the pen when I saw the butcher van pull into our driveway, which was a good hundred yards away from the pen. And to my surprise, Wally and Beaver immediately went bat-shit. They knew something was up. They ran around the pen squealing like I'd never seen. They'd never seen the butcher or his van. And *they're pigs,* yet they were visibly rattled as this guy barreled toward their quarters. His rig pulled to a stop just outside the last gate. He got out of his truck with a .22-caliber pistol and popped each pig in the head. He then slit their throats to bleed them out, hung 'em up, gutted 'em, skinned 'em, chainsawed them both down the middle and put them in his refrigerated truck, and drove off.

That was the moment when I realized there are going to be some things in life that will blow your hair back even though they'll be clearly stated on the list of things to do that day. And in this case, there was a world of difference in knowing that animals get slaughtered for food and witnessing it firsthand.

A week later, a portion of the meat was delivered to our house. My mother had cooked up some of the bacon and put it on the table for breakfast. I took a bite, and although it was arguably the best bacon I had ever tasted up until that point, I had a hard time turning the corner and not feeling as if I was snacking on a family pet.

Pork remains my favorite meat to this day. I have a butcher near where I live, and I'm a regular customer. In the end, I'm just more comfortable not knowing whom I'll be eating. It's better that way. For both of us.

The Sign

Caitlin Roper

I was twelve, flushed cheek pressed against the backseat window of my mom's car. It was hot and humid, a dense, damp haze pressing down on everything. Even the trees were wilting. I wanted to be anywhere but there, in New England, in a car with my family. We'd just crossed the Connecticut River heading toward the Vermont border from northwestern Massachusetts. I had grown up in Northern California, and this was my first summer living with my mom and stepfather in southern Vermont. I didn't like it.

My parents had shared custody of me since their divorce, when I was a toddler. I spent one week with each for years, back and forth between two very different homes in Berkeley, California. At my father's house I was an only child; he worked at home, and we got along well. My dad lived in an apartment in a nice neighborhood in the hills. At my mom's, things were a little less predictable, and much more difficult. There was more conflict, and I had more responsibility, looking after myself and my little sister. My mom lived in a Victorian house in a bad neighborhood. I went back and forth, week after week, shuttling, alone, between two environments. I had two sets of friends, two commutes, two lives. I changed schools six times before I reached high school.

When I started eighth grade, my mom, stepdad, and little sister moved to Guilford, Vermont. I was asked to choose. Would I rather move to Vermont or stay in Berkeley? I pretended to consider my decision. I stayed with my dad. But that meant I had to spend a few months of the summer in Vermont.

On this oppressively hot day, trapped in the backseat, I watched the green landscape blur past as I thought about how much I wished I was home in California. The foliage lining Route 9 gave way to lawn, and there it was, a sign—an actual sign—for Northfield Mt. Hermon School, founded 1879. The sign was a horizontal oval shape, carved in wood, the name of the school wrapped around what looked like a genie's lamp. The sign marked the entrance to the school, but all I could see was a road leading back into the woods. The idea of a school where students lived, on their own, down a shady wooded street, was mysterious, novel, and enchanting.

As soon as I could, I went to the library and looked up "boarding school" in the card catalog. I found a reference guide to private secondary schools and looked up "Northfield Mt. Hermon" in the index. Soon after, I wrote away for an application. With a scholarship, I convinced my freethinking, self-employed artist parents that boarding school was not only for rich folks who wanted to get rid of their kids. At fourteen, after a cross-country road trip with my dad, I entered NMH as a sophomore. I'd spend the summers in Berkeley. Boarding school turned me on to learning, and changed the course of my life. But the single most important realization of my life was that I could determine my own fate, that a change of circumstance was always within reach, just outside the window.

The Thin Envelope

Sascha Rothchild

My father went to Yale. He never pressured me into follow-ing in his footsteps but instead just regaled me with fabu-lous collegiate stories about the intoxicating songs of the Whiffen-poofs, the late nights at the *Yale Daily News*, and the mysterious and powerful secret societies: Scroll and Key, Spade and Grave, and Skull and Bones. While other kids were learning to tie their shoes I was dreaming of a life amid the gothic and Georgian buildings, the ivy, and the other incredibly smart people. I would major in theater, of course.

I wore Yale T-shirts with a certain smugness usually reserved for people getting their master's in social work and by sophomore year of high school had proudly placed a bumper sticker on my car. A tradition usually reserved for senior year once you knew for sure where you were going. But I knew I was going to Yale. It wasn't just my first choice; it was my *only* choice. With all AP classes, nearly per-fect grades, diverse extracurricular activities, brilliant essays, and, of course, being a legacy, I thought I was a shoo-in.

It was mid-December when the envelope arrived.

I had confidently applied early admission. I was milling about the kitchen, my future still bright, when I saw the post lady walk up our driveway. I excitedly bounded outside to meet her and went through the stack of mail. Then I saw it. It was thin. Not only thin but small. A regular-sized envelope. Not the big folder filled with cheery glossy pictures of students in the quad, dorm room info, and commissary eating options.

Ashamed and angry I stormed over to my car and tried to rip off the bumper sticker but the Miami heat had melded it to the rubber and it wouldn't budge. The blue and white YALE glared at me as if to say, "That's what you get for your hubris, silly girl." My father walked out of the house as I sat down on the driveway, defeated. "I didn't get in," I said. In this moment I realized I could want something so completely, try my very best, work really hard, and still fail.

I also realized, although I was sitting in a fetal position, that I was still standing, so to speak. I was still alive and breathing and failure hadn't killed me. There was something liberating in this knowledge. I could try lots of things and fail many times and my future was still bright, and full of safety schools.

Liner Notes

Elizabeth Jayne Liu

am running away. I want you to have my CDs. Don't scratch them."

What did I know as an eighteen-year-old? I knew that I was pregnant. I knew that I was going to be a single mother. I knew that my parents wanted me to terminate my pregnancy. If I could just withstand their incessant prodding for five more weeks, I would pass the six-month mark, and the procedure would be illegal. I knew that I was running away. As soon as my best friend pulled into the driveway, I knew I would be without a home, without any money and without a plan for the next five weeks.

I had made the decision to run away the day before. I didn't have to wait long for my chance. As soon as my mother left for the grocery store, I quickly called my best friend and packed two garbage bags. With a teenager's lack of forethought, I stuffed every pair of shoes I owned into one bag and three sweatshirts into the other plastic bag. I didn't pack a clean change of underwear or any pants.

The only possessions I had given any thought to were my CDs. Every last cent I'd earned from odd jobs went into purchasing those

CDs. They represented all my careless adventures and frivolous youthful indulgences.

I never let anyone touch them, but I knew I couldn't bring them along. They would get lost or stolen while I shuffled around from one place to another, so I decided to leave them to my brother. But I didn't trust him, and I couldn't just leave them on his desk, lest the significance was lost on a sixteen-year-old. I decided to write a note:

"I am running away. I want you to have my CDs. Don't scratch them."

In that moment, as I wrote that note, I knew I was leaving behind any vestige of youth. I was stepping into adulthood.

I walked out of my childhood home with two garbage bags. As the car drove farther and farther away, I couldn't help but turn around and look one last time.

"He better not wreck those CDs."

I never lived in that home again.

My daughter, Calyx, recently turned eleven.

If I Don't Die Today, I Will Marry Kristin Moore

Aaron Huey

The day we were ambushed by the Taliban, I was wearing a forty-five-pound flak jacket but no helmet. The jacket weighed me down as I ran through empty villages, choking on fear, far from the Dyncorp mercenaries we came with. Major Khalil was screaming into his radio as we raced deeper into the battle, a captured Taliban prisoner in tow. As I ran, the poppies coated my pants with raw opium stains. Later, lying in a ditch with my writer, Jon Lee Anderson, and our translators, I prayed for an air strike. In that moment I stopped caring about collateral damage, I just wanted them to raze that village to the ground. And again, when I was crawling through a muddy field while Afghan Eradication Forces (AEF) and Taliban fighters exchanged gunfire across the tops of the bleeding plants, I remember distinctly not giving a shit about my cameras, *The New Yorker*, or my career.

I do remember holding Jon Lee's hand over the seat of our Ford F250 as bullets rained down in that orchard. I told him I was scared. He said he knew. I'd said it many times that day. I told him this time it was different.

"I'm *really* scared," I said.

He reached over the seat and held my hand.

The shooting had started three hours ago, and we had no clear exit. In the backseat of our unarmored Ford F250 there was a translator and a Dyncorp medic. I pressed down between them as close to the floor as I could so that they would absorb the bullets. At some point a helicopter arrived and raked both sides of the road with thousands of fifty-caliber rounds before being hit and retreating to base. It was a sweet sound at the time, like plastic wrappers crackling in your hand as you wad them into a ball. I have to admit I wanted more. I wanted all of it to be blown to fucking hell. So I could walk away.

Jon Lee reminded me to keep shooting pictures. I really didn't care about the pictures anymore. I wasn't worried enough about

getting blurry shots of trees to offer myself up for target practice. At the river, a truck was stuck and we were trapped on the bank, surrounded on all sides but for one narrow escape route. Five mercenaries stood along the bank and in the water, full-on Rambo. They fought from behind ATVs and our unarmored trucks. They were calm. They were at work.

I was on a riverbank, huddled up under the wheel well. Jon Lee is a pretty casual guy. He knew we were in deep shit, but he also knew that panicking wouldn't help us.

"A husband tells his wife," Jon Lee started in, "'I bet you can't tell me something that makes me happy and sad at the same time.' 'Your brother has a small dick,' she says." He'd already told me this one, but it was a little funnier in the middle of an ambush. I cracked a weak smile. The Taliban were closing in and starting to surround us. We were four hours into this thing, and every time I thought it was going to end, every time the shooting stopped, it began again, doubled in intensity, and grew exponentially more horrifying and inescapable.

I want to tell you what it was really like to think death is imminent, but I can't. It's a taste in your mouth. And an emptiness. I imagined myself on YouTube with a knife to my throat. *Allah O Akbar.*

I was thinking about not being me anymore. About not having a body. About the things I did wrong. But mostly I was thinking about a girl.

I'd been stringing her along for five years. *What an asshole. Why am I waiting for her to change? Why am I such a fucking coward? Selfish fuck.* We almost got married three times.

I am going to die here. I didn't think about my family or my friends. I didn't think about home or my dog. I thought about Kristin. All she wanted, all that she would ever want, was for me to see her as she is, to love her cleanly and all the way through. I'd been so busy loving myself.

When it ended two men were dead, and I was not one of them.

Back in Kabul:

The Jalalabad road east of the city leads past an Afghan military base. Behind that base there is a field of metal carcasses. It is a graveyard for tanks, APCs, and jeeps. It is quiet there; few places in Kabul are.

I told Kristin we were going there to take photos. On the trail that leads across the grassy field through the tanks, she was afraid we would step on a land mine. I chose a tank to sit on and showed her a small red box with two gold rings inside. Kristin shrugged and smiled.

"Sure," she said. "Right now?"

"Yes."

Jon Lee was ordained on the Internet the night before, and read a page of vows I'd written. Our driver and translator had never seen a man and woman kiss before. They blushed and turned away. The rings were cheap, and we sold them back to a jeweler the next day.

Kristin Moore is my wife.

Thank you, Taliban.

@KatrinaNation: "Moment that changed my life was being hijacked in 1978. Made me a journalist."
—*Katrina vanden Heuvel, editor of* The Nation, *via Twitter*

Boot Camp

Wes Moore

I was twelve years old and had just earned my Cap Shield at the military school that I'd been forced to attend. We had just completed, "Plebe System," which was the first six weeks of the school—a completion I didn't think I'd ever see. When I began my time at Valley Forge Military Academy, I was full of anger and fear, with a good dose of apathy thrown in. I'd been sent because, at critical junctures in my life, I'd regularly made wrong decisions. I'd tried my mother's patience on multiple occasions. Finally her patience had run out.

Completing that six-week "boot camp" for new cadets at the school was the first thing that I felt I'd accomplished on my own. I'd been a king of excuses, consistently coming up with reasons why I didn't accomplish assignments or follow basic rules and laws. Now I'd come to realize that excuses are the tools of the incompetent, and that I needed to step up to survive. At twelve years old, I stood up straight and smiled as they presented me my Cap Shield, the small brass symbol that represented completion of the Plebe System. But that shiny token meant much more; it symbolized irreversible growth.

Sunset Strip

Christine MacDonald

I rolled down my window, giving the warm Waikiki air permission to sweep across my lap, hoping to wipe the trace of cigarette smoke from the back seat of the cab. As the breeze tickled my face, I rifled through my duffle bag.

Shoes: check. Make-up: check.

My fingers grazed the small of my back.

G-string: check.

We stopped at a light just four blocks from the club and I took in the view. The sun was already tucked in to the blue ocean for the night, and the sky above the horizon was cloaked in hues of lavender and tangerine. The stoplight turned green and we continued up the street, then turned down a narrow unpaved driveway and stopped in front of the club.

I could tell the top girls were working. I didn't mind sharing the stage with centerfolds; it made me feel like one, in a way. The room was packed, but I made my way to the bar. I threw a five down and ordered my usual vodka and cranberry.

"Ladies and gentlemen, give it up for Niki, Donna, and Amberrrrrrr!"

The crowd was cheering. I opened the dressing room door with one hand, balancing my drink and bag with the other. I managed to find a seat next to the mirror and settled in, trying to tune out the other girls as I pulled out my makeup case.

I squeezed the flesh-colored liquid on my finger, wiping my cheeks slowly. Spackle—to cover every acne scar. My skin was uneven like melted wax, always haunting me with the memories of name-calling and humiliation. After filling every crevice, I let out a sigh of acceptance and validation. I showed them.

"All right, all right, all right! Give it up!"

The door opened and another dancer arrived. She was young—a new girl. Someone I'd never seen before. We surveyed one another, and she made her way past me.

Suddenly, I shut my eyes. I saw Michelle, with her scabbed arms and caked-on makeup, talking about her daughter while taking a drag from a cigarette. I saw Cassandra, and the look on her face when I told her that her boyfriend had made a pass at me. I saw the wrinkled pixie who worked as a fortune-teller by day. I heard Kami, yelling at a customer who had tried to touch her. I smelled Loretta, the pot-smoking beauty who came to town twice a year. I saw Billy and Billy, the male and female striptease act who liked to party and swing. I saw Robert, offering me mountains of cocaine, while using me for a place to stay.

The heavy bass of the next song vibrated the walls, and my eyes opened to my own reflection in the mirror. I saw myself, a twenty-eight-year-old stripper. Studying my eyes, I discovered that what used to be pools of blue were now dull shades of gray. Nothing scared me more than the realization that I was the architect of my own demise. What was once a fantasy of fame and fortune had become a harsh reality of reputation and endurance.

Perhaps seeing the new girl made me realize I wasn't nineteen anymore. Nearly a decade in the making, my career as a stripper felt weathered. I wanted to live a normal life. I didn't know what that meant exactly, but it suddenly hit me: I wasn't going to find it on stage. I spoke softly to the woman with the tired, gray eyes: "I think you're done."

I took another sip from my drink and stood up. I brushed past the new girl, wondering if she felt my urge to hug her. I wanted to tell her to save her money and not get caught up in the nightlife, but instead I said, "Have a good night," and kept walking.

My head floating in a sea of uncertainty, I made my way through the crowd. I pulled open the red velvet curtains at the front door and saw that the sky was a deep purple.

I always looked at sunsets as beginnings: the beginning of my shift and a night out. But that early-evening sky marked the opposite—an end to a life I no longer wanted or needed. Tomorrow would be a new day.

Truth, Lies, and Audiotape

Dan Baum

found him in Atlanta, doing minority recruitment for an engineering firm after serving a stint in federal prison, and John Ehrlichman looked nothing like he had on television twenty years earlier.

It was 1992, and I was starting work on a book about the politics of drug prohibition. I was much under the sway of Randy Shilts's *And the Band Played On* and intended to structure my book similarly. Mine would be built as the *story*—with a beginning, middle, and end; characters and dialogue; entirely told "in scene"—of how drugs had been transformed from a minor public health problem into a devastating political weapon.

Ehrlichman, Richard Nixon's advisor for domestic affairs and one of the main Watergate conspirators, was one of the people I most wanted to interview. He was a genuine villain of American history; we don't often get to meet them.

He was much shorter than I expected—fat, with a gigantic mountain-man beard. As I started asking him earnest, wonky questions about Nixon's drug policy, he held up a hand to stop me. "You want to know what this was really all about?" he asked with the weariness of a man who no longer had anything to protect. "The Nixon campaign in 1968, and the Nixon White House after that, had two enemies: the antiwar Left, and black people. You understand what I'm saying? We knew we couldn't make it illegal to be either against the war or black. But by getting the public to associate the hippies with marijuana and blacks with heroin, and then criminalizing both heavily, we could disrupt those communities. We could arrest their leaders, raid their homes, break up their meetings, and vilify them night after night on the evening news. Did we know we were lying about the drugs? Of course we did."

It may have been the first time in my career as a reporter that I'd been given an entirely straight answer. It changed everything about the way I conducted all the other interviews for my book—and, really, for all the interviews I've done since then. Just as Woodward and Bernstein taught me that any story can be gotten, Ehrlichman taught me that people really do understand what truly motivates them, and that, if asked in the right way, they'll discuss it. I've been grateful to that conniving bastard ever since.

Stage Direction

Saïd Sayrafiezadeh

The first time I encountered Samuel Beckett's *Krapp's Last Tape,* I was supremely uninterested. The occasion was an initial read-through in a small, bare-bones Pittsburgh theater that was producing an evening of short Beckett plays, one of which I had been cast in. I was twenty-three years old at the time and had an outsized sense of my acting ability as well as what the future held in store for me. Meanwhile, I was enduring a dreary existence, chronically single, jobless, antisocial—with the exception of theater—and living alone on the outskirts of the city. I was convinced that things were about to change for me at any moment and that all I had to do was wait and be patient.

There was a nagging awareness, however, that if there was any hope of altering my life, artistically and emotionally, I had to move to New York City. I had been contemplating this for several years, but I was paralyzed by the prospect of leaving a city in which I had lived almost all of my life and that had become so familiar and comforting. Instead, I decided to continue to wait and be patient.

So on a cold night in January of 1992, I sat with five other actors and read aloud from the plays that would comprise our evening of

Beckett. I had been cast in *Rough for Theater I* in which I played an energetic and conniving invalid who gets to roll around in a wheelchair duping a blind man. I liked my play. In fact, I liked all of the plays except for *Krapp's Last Tape,* which struck me as convoluted and pointless. It was a forty-five-minute story about nothing but an old man named Krapp who listens to a tape recording he made of himself thirty years earlier.

Four weeks of rehearsals passed. I was still single—and still waiting. The night before we opened we were afforded an opportunity to sit in the audience and watch the other plays, the last of which was *Krapp's Last Tape.* It began with the thirty-nine-year-old actor, impressively made up to look ancient, staring out at the audience from behind a desk that held a tape recorder. Above him a lone light bulb dangled. This was succeeded by ten wordless minutes of banana eating that was absolutely hilarious. I laughed aloud in the empty theater. And after that the story proper began, with the elderly Krapp listening to the tape recording he had made on his birthday, thirty years earlier.

Suddenly it was no longer funny. The juxtaposition of the recording and the solitary old man in his dark apartment was sobering and unsettling. It was evident that the owner of the young voice on the tape had a rather grand view of himself and his possibilities while we, the audience, were given to understand that what had ultimately resulted thirty years later were missed opportunities, lost love, and abject isolation. Beckett's message was simple: *time will pass.* Sitting in the audience, I thought about how I was only twenty-three years old, but that one day, much sooner than I expected, I would be thirty-three years old, and then I would be forty-three, and so on, and that it was quite possible that I would end up, in my old age, exactly the person I was now, living alone in Pittsburgh, dreaming of change, and wondering what would have happened if I had moved to New York City.

"Perhaps my best years are gone. When there was a chance at happiness," the young recorded Krapp says at the close of the play, his vain, pompous tone barely diminished. "But I wouldn't want them back. Not with the fire in me now. No, I wouldn't want them back." And with the tape machine running on in silence, the old Krapp stares out at the audience, a look of defeat and horror, as I stared back.

Perhaps this play would not have affected me so much if not for the fact that for the next three weeks, three nights each week, I was forced to sit in the dressing room in my theatrically distressed suit and listen to it again and again, until every one of Beckett's heartbreaking words had been committed to memory. And each night when the monologue was nearing its end, I would stand in the wings for the curtain call, and I would watch that closing moment, now seared forever into my brain, with Krapp staring out at the audience and the disembodied voice intoning, "Perhaps my best years are gone. When there was a chance of happiness."

The following year I was living in New York City.

February 12, 2009, 9:14 a.m.

Daniel DiClerico

In the master bedroom of my parents' home, gray morning light slants through the picture window looking out over leafless woods. My father felled some forty dead or dying trees in recent years, carving a clear view to the Green Mountain foothills on the far side of Quechee Valley. Right now, though, he's gone for donuts.

It's his first time out of the house in a week. When I arrived from work the Thursday prior, the three-hundred-mile commute made in record time, he was seated bedside. From the driveway, I watched him lean forward, saw his head dip beneath the windowsill before rising up a few beats later. I knew then that I was too late.

Only I wasn't. Through days and nights we waited. More than once I heard my father's footfalls in the early morning hours. From the top of the stairs, he called to his children. "It's time." Only it wasn't. There were more turnings and washings and dressings, even a flicker of hope after a sudden movement in the shower. My father phoned the doctor. "We're not getting our hopes up here," he insisted.

My father hung up the phone and requested some broth. There were no cans in the cupboard, so we made do with a frozen chicken breast and some limp carrots and celery stalks. A few spoonfuls of the watery liquid went down. The rest went cold on the back burner. My father returned to his chair.

"Is she waiting for someone?" the hospice nurse asked. She'd taken a special interest in our case since learning that the patient was one of her own, a fellow Charon in paisley-patterned scrubs who for decades ferried her own terminally ill through their final hours. Or days, as the case may be. And was.

"No," we said. "We're all here."

The vigil went on. Time unraveled, circadian rhythms stopped. Sleep here, sleep there, sweatpants at dinner, whiskey at dawn. Until, finally, this.

I'm seated at the desk in the bedroom of my parent's home. To my left, the gray morning light. To my right, my dying mother.

But first, back twenty-five years. I'm standing in the front room of my childhood home in suburban New Jersey, hidden behind the half-drawn Venetian blinds. It's my nightly post, as evidenced by the patch of frayed carpet at my feet. Finally, the headlights of my mother's maroon Honda Accord turn into the driveway. I make a beeline for the TV room and listen as the car door slams. She climbs the back steps and calls out in a singsong voice "Helloooo. . . . Anyone home?" I want to run to her, but I'm a pubescent scrum of hormones and discomfort, so I barely grunt hello when she pops her head in.

"Danny," my eldest sister now says. She's taken my father's place in the bedside chair. I turn to her, turn to the deathbed, just as my mother's body jerks my way. Her gaze lands on me. Our eyes lock. There's one final rattle deep from within. Then silence.

That's when I know that death, even when you most expect it, is a surprise. But also that, unless it's your own, life goes on.

"What time is it?" my sister asks.

"Nine fourteen," I say, looking to the alarm clock on the bedside table.

"Will you tell Dad?" she asks, holding our mother's left hand.

"Okay," I say, and get up to hold the other.

"I turn to her, turn to the deathbed, just as my mother's body jerks my way. Her gaze lands on me. Our eyes lock."

Balls Out

James Cañón

I was twenty-five years old and about to leave Colombia, and my four brothers still didn't know I was gay. I had tried to tell them many times before, but when the moment came, I always felt I couldn't. I'd convinced myself that coming out to them would be a mistake; that they didn't need to know. Not just then, anyway, when I was going to America for a year to learn English. There, for twelve whole months, I wouldn't have to go out on dates with the girls my brothers introduced me to; wouldn't have to pretend that I liked to play soccer and watch videos of busty women mud wrestling.

I'll tell them next year, I said to myself, when I return to Bogotá. I had also convinced myself that I was going to return.

The week before I left, I took Lukas, our six-year-old dog, to the vet clinic to get neutered. The procedure, the vet had advised us, would eliminate the possibility of testicular tumors and reduce the risk of prostate disease, both common problems in male dogs over the age of five. After the surgery, the vet told me Lukas would have to stay in the clinic overnight for observation. He gave me Lukas's testicles in a small jar. They looked like sushi balls. I put the jar in my backpack and went home.

That night, I took the jar out and showed it to my brothers, holding it in my cupped hands, like something precious. They looked at it, making all sorts of comments and expressions of disgust. Finally, one of them said, "Wonder what it feels like to hold someone else's balls in your hands?"

My brothers were laughing. It was just a joke, of course, not directed at me, but even so I felt the familiar panic rising in my body as I watched them. And then I looked down at the contents of the jar, and my panic evaporated, replaced by a sense of power I'd never known before.

"I'm gay," I shouted over their raucous laughter.

The room grew quiet. My brothers, all four of them, looked at me with raised eyebrows, waiting for me to tell them I was joking.

"I'm gay," I repeated. "As in homosexual."

There was no need for lengthy explanations. There was nothing to explain. Oscar and Hernán, my two oldest brothers, seemed calm and resigned, as if they'd already known. Pepe, the one who had made the joke, was confused and embarrassed. And predictably, Carlos, the youngest, sat on the sofa and wept.

I left for New York the following week, and my absence gave my brothers time to process my news. I never went back to Colombia except to visit, and yet my relationship with them has grown stronger over the years, because it's now based on honesty and openness. Because I don't have to hide anymore.

Lukas gained weight and became lazy, but he never lost his zest for life. He lived to be seventeen. As for his balls, I visit them every time I go home. I buried them in the backyard and set a cross to mark the spot where they lie.

You never know when you'll need an extra pair.

Marooned

Kristen Cosby

My brother and I grew up before the mast, deckhands aboard the thirty-nine-foot sailboat that my father and mother built in our backyard. Before I was a daughter, I was a member of a crew captained by my father and made up of my mother, younger brother, and a fat black mutt. We launched the year I was seven, and divided our lives between worlds: work and school ashore, and adventure on the sea. Pressed together in the single cabin for months at a time, we roved up and down the eastern seaboard, training to cross oceans. I learned to man the helm the year I was eight, to stand watch alone the year I was nine. At fourteen, I could operate the entire ship. We explored Nova Scotia, Newfoundland, Chesapeake Bay, Bermuda, Florida, Georgia, the Hudson, and every cranny of the Gulf of Maine.

Now, from the safety of my adult life ashore, I swagger, bragging about my toughness, my capabilities, but living aboard for much of my childhood made me an exile, different from other kids at school in a way they could feel, but not name. In the town where I went to school, where four generations of my family lived, I became a foreigner.

I resented our rough, weird lifestyle. I wanted to wear dresses (forbidden aboard), ride a bicycle into town, and buy ice cream with friends.

By the summer I was sixteen, I'd had enough. I had my first job, hosting at a restaurant in a town on Penobscot Bay, a few miles by water from where we moored for the summer. I packed a knapsack of clothes, a crate of books, and dried goods. My father and mother ferried me ashore and helped me carry my things to a cabin we'd built over the high-tide line on an acre of land rented from friends. The cabin was twelve by sixteen feet and furnished with a bunk, a wood stove, and a kerosene lantern. Behind it was a state park, a wilderness that stretched for miles with a single dirt road cut through it. For the rest of the summer, I would access civilization—my job, groceries, human company—by skiff. I'd haul water in jugs and bags from a nearby spring or from the town dock next to the restaurant.

Inside the cabin, I doubled-checked the lanterns for fuel. At sixteen, I was afraid of the forest behind the cabin, how it limited my vision, how dark it was at night.

"We'll be back," my mother said as she set down my crate of books, oatmeal, and raisins. We had no cell-phones, or hand-held radios. Over the coming weeks, we'd be out of contact. My father and mother hopped back into the dinghy and motored out to the ship. For the next half hour, I watched the crew—my family—ready our ship without me. They raised sail, dropped mooring, and turned the bow of my home toward the mouth of the cove, and headed out to sea.

I grabbed the binoculars and watched the last corner of sail disappear around the headlands.

The dangers I'd have to navigate, traveling by water alone at night after my shift at the restaurant, riding out storms in a shake and plywood shack, and hiking over rough paths where injury would be easy and deadly, didn't occur to me. I was sixteen and immortal. What gut-punched me was loneliness. As if looking through water, the present stilled and I could see clearly into our future. Our paths would diverge from this moment. My parents and brother would go to sea, live aboard year-round, sail around the world, and I would not.

The tide would come in under the cabin and retreat to the ocean, leaving the land bare. I felt no pull toward one or the other, only a sense of unease. I was deeply afraid of what was to come—that I'd die alone, in the distant future, wandering across the mainland, unmoored and without the ability to grow roots. My life aboard had ended.

When I returned to the vessel, I would be changed—less obedient, full of ideas about myself as an individual, separate from the crew. That fierce individualism would create both the fuel and the need to run—first from them, and then from place to place, seeking an equally raw and beautiful country to which I could belong. But that first day, as the vessel disappeared, the fuel for my rebellion drained from me. I stood alone on the beach, alone, wondering if I'd made the right choice.

Meeting Allen Ginsberg

Steve Silberman

On February 4, 1977, I was eighteen and in New York City with my first boyfriend—a beautiful, blue-eyed kid named Ed. We were on an unofficial break from Oberlin College in Ohio. Fresh off a Greyhound bus, I plucked a copy of the *Village Voice* from a street corner box. A listing inside revealed that poet Allen Ginsberg was reading at Queens College that night.

Growing up in a Jewish, antiwar radical household, I was no stranger to the name Ginsberg. My academic new-Left parents viewed him as a frivolous distraction, cavorting in Indian *schmattes*, promoting pot smoking and homosexuality (both merely symptoms of the inevitable decline of state capitalism), and chanting "Om" at the Chicago Democratic convention—while the *real* revolutionaries were getting their heads bashed in.

But having enjoyed such poems as "A Supermarket in California" in high school English classes, and being a *fegeleh* myself, I was eager to see the bearded guru in person. That evening, Ed and I jumped on a subway to Queens and took seats in the front row of the auditorium.

The author (front) and poets Allen Ginsberg (back left) and Marc Olmsted. *Photograph courtesy of Marc Geller.*

Allen came onstage and gave an inspired reading that climaxed with a performance of William Blake's "The Nurse's Song," for which he had written his own music. At fifty-one, the poet was bald, with white hairs sprouting out of his ears; he was dressed like a professor, in a frayed Oxford shirt and tie. Instead of a raving Beat madman, he looked like my uncle at the deli.

At the same time, I had never seen a middle-aged guy so willing to be transported by ecstasy. There was an angelic-looking kid my age named Steven Taylor seated next to him onstage, accompanying Allen on guitar while singing harmonies in a high, pure, aching tenor. I didn't know if the poet and the boy were together or not, but they were obviously in love, exchanging mutually delighted glances as Blake's lyric unspooled after the last verse into a spiraling mantra.

"And all the hills echoed," they sang together, enunciating the last word as three syllables—*ech-o-wed*—Allen's cantorial exhalations marrying Steven's golden tones in a public proclamation of joy.

Though Allen was not my "type," I fell instantly in love. I made a vow to myself that wherever the poet would be that summer, I would find him and do anything I could to make his life better. I would rent an apartment across the street (wherever he lived), run errands to the grocery store, do his laundry, whatever.

Fast forward to June, to a crowded auditorium in Boulder, Colorado, home of Naropa Institute, a Buddhist college where Allen taught "The Literary History of the Beat Generation" in the summer. I had sent away for a catalog and swooned over the course offerings: William Burroughs on screenwriting using Gregory Corso's "Socratic Rap." (Never mind that Burroughs knew little about screenwriting—he was charming and funny—and that Corso's rap consisted of him soliciting joints from students while uttering home-brewed koans like, "What are fish? *Animalized water!*")

I had sold everything I owned and hopped on a train to Colorado in hopes of earning an apprenticeship with Ginsberg. I got no response to my application letter, but when I introduced myself to Allen in person, he said, "Oh, you wrote me that very nice letter." I got the apprenticeship.

In truth, that first summer with Allen was awkward. His father had just died. Allen was freaked out about mortality, short-tempered, rude to students he wasn't attracted to, and hornier than ever. (Now that I'm a year older than Allen was then, and my own father and first boyfriend are dead, I understand where he was coming from.)

But it was also the summer that my whole life changed.

I committed myself to writing full-time, which I still do for a living. Ten years later, I would return to Naropa as Allen's teaching assistant. An old Zen master showed me how to meditate and I became a Buddhist.

The summer of 1977 was the summer that I became me.

And later, when I told an old friend of Jack Kerouac's—the poet and Zen teacher Philip Whalen—that my first few months with Allen Ginsberg had been disillusioning, he replied, "What's so great about illusions anyway?"

Those Old Keys

Alan Cheuse

If it weren't for one moment in my childhood, I might say that it was the moment I met my first wife at a party in New York City or the moment I met my second wife at a business meeting (also) in New York or the moment I met my third and present (and last, I pray) wife at an artists' colony in northern California. These moments made for years of struggle, but pleasure also, the continuing pleasure of fathering three children, now grown, and the companionship that writers need to keep their inherently isolated life from going sour.

But the defining moment that came long before any of these? I must have been four or five when I first heard my father clacking away on the keys of an old Remington typewriter. I ventured near, to inquire about what he was doing, and like the victim of a vortex out of Poe or a black hole out of astrophysics, I was drawn in, and still spin around in the sound of the keyboard, his, and mine.

Mission Accomplished

Brian Evenson

Roughly twenty years ago, I was a Mormon missionary serving in Wisconsin. I lived in a small apartment with five other missionaries. Mormon missionaries are always supposed to be in the company of their companions; there's never a moment of pure solitude. You're also not allowed to read anything but the scriptures or approved religious texts, nor listen to "inappropriate" music, nor watch movies. After a while you forget what the real world is like.

I used to wake up at three or four in the morning and sneak outside. I'd sit on the steps in the stairwell for fifteen or twenty minutes, relishing those few minutes to myself. Sometimes I'd read Robert Pinget's *Charrue*, which for some reason was one of the few non-religious books I had and which nobody had encouraged me to give up since it was written in French. Other times I'd just look out over the parking lot. Often by the time I went back inside, someone would be awake and ask me to explain where I'd been. Or someone would bring up my absence casually over breakfast the next morning.

Eventually I reached the point where I couldn't stand it anymore but didn't know how to get out. I was worried about what my relatives would think and knew it would cause complications for me when it came time to be readmitted to Brigham Young University, the Mormon college I'd been going to before leaving on a mission.

One day I went into the mission office where I worked. As I walked to the bathroom, I suddenly thought, *What if I leave now and never come back?* A little shaken, I went back to work as usual, but the thought kept returning. A few days later, I excused myself to use the bathroom again and instead walked down the hall and just kept going. Once out of the building, I ran the half mile or so to my apartment. I called some friends and asked if they could pick me up, changed out of my white shirt and tie, and tossed as many of my belongings as would fit into a duffle bag. And then I left, cutting across a park to the spot where my friend was to pick me up. From where I waited, I saw my Mormon companions' car pull into the parking lot of our apartment building and several missionaries rush in, apparently looking for me.

And then my friend pulled up.

Two hours later, the mission president had tracked me down and telephoned my friend's house to plead with me to come back. This was not the right way to leave, he told me. If I wanted to leave I needed to come do it officially. I only had a few months of my mission left: it would be a shame to throw everything away. I needed to sit down with him and have a serious chat. And maybe after having that chat, he suggested, I'd see how wrong I'd been.

No, I said. It was the first time in a long while I'd felt as if I was making a decision for myself. In fact, I was shocked when the mission president called and my friend left the room to respect my privacy. There had been no real privacy or consideration of that sort for months.

The mission president marshaled his forces. Didn't I know this decision, made in an instant, would have a permanent effect on my life? I did, but I took responsibility for those decisions. My parents called to ask if I was willing to reconsider. I told them no. One of my religious leaders from home called. I again said no.

It's arguably pathological, but I've come to feel that it was through these simple acts of blunt refusal, my making a choice and taking responsibility for it and any consequences, that I became who I am. And, perhaps more importantly, I became sure of who I am.

Tell Me How This Ends

Patrick Callahan

Lots of hospitalizations."

This was my son's future as foretold by his doctor, famous in our family for his Javier Bardem, *No Country for Old Men*, bedside manner. I had called him from my kitchen to arrange medical attention for my son, after my wife, Jean, brought Sean back from seeing his pediatrician and told me, exhausted, that our youngest boy, then ten, had juvenile diabetes.

And *this* was the good doctor's response: "Whatever fleeting plans you thought you had for a normal family life, with two mentally disabled sons, forget it. You thought you had problems, pal? Yesterday was the good old days."

And there was the moment, standing at our kitchen sink, the doctor's disembodied voice speaking of future heartbreak, when I added up the score and asked myself:

How are we going to pull this off?
Sean's ten years old.
He's Fragile X and nonverbal.

He can't tell us when his sugar level is too low or too high or when he
feels faint or sick.
He only eats pretzels and waffles now, for God's sake.
How are we going to keep this boy alive?

Jean and I are sometimes asked why the boys' Fragile X disability
didn't make us angry or resentful—the whole "why us?" thing. The
answer was, and is, things happen—that's the way it is, although I
do often bite my tongue when listening to friends speak of terrible
family traumas like sprained ankles, a bad prom date, or perhaps a
child getting only half a scholarship to Penn State. Such problems are
fleeting, I want to say, as Sean gets his fifth shot of six daily needles.

Sometimes I think back to that phone conversation, particularly
on late nights when Jean is utterly spent, asleep on the couch in the
family room, and I hear Sean get up above us and come down the
stairs to the kitchen. He'll sit down at his place at the table, silently
telling me he's low (blood sugar) and needs to eat. He'll eat pretzel
rods and drink milk in that same kitchen where twelve years ago I had
that moment, the dark other side of what my doctor was really saying.

That I might have to bury my boy.

Keepsake

Jennifer Egan

In the summer of 1981, at the tail end of a year off between high school and college, I flew to Europe alone, with a backpack and a Eurail pass, determined to cure my absurd lack of worldliness in one grand voyage. Two weeks into the trip, I began having panic attacks that I mistook for drug flashbacks (having read, like the rest of my generation, *Go Ask Alice*), which I feared were a first step toward real insanity. I stuck it out a few more weeks, but eventually called my mother, weeping, from Rome, and went home early. And yet it was during that short time in Europe that I decided to become a writer.

Recently, I returned to my leatherbound journal in search of the moment when this revelation took place. But if there was a *moment*, I'd failed to record it. What strikes me, rereading those pages for the first time in many years, is how happy I sound at times. Maybe, having worked and saved for most of my year off to pay for the trip, I couldn't bear to admit (even to myself) that it was evolving into a nightmare. Maybe I've forgotten how much genuine happiness was commingled with the fear. But I suspect it was the fact that writing in the journal *made* me happy— even when the experiences I described were frightening or desperate.

I'd stumbled on the sheer pleasure of writing, and it's been with me ever since.

Following are some annotated snippets from the diary:

5/17/81 [San Francisco, days before departure]

I can't decide whether I'm unusual because I'm one of the few who even analyzes myself to this extent, or whether the analyzation [sic] is merely a result of dissatisfaction which most people just don't feel.

5/31/81 London

I adore paintings. They're little windows into other worlds, or other peoples' perceptions of their worlds. It's the closest you can get to living someone else's life. Through paintings you see their world through their vision. Now of course you see their vision through your own, but that's unavoidable.

I think I'll go to Copenhagen for one night after Holland. I CAN'T BELIEVE I CAN REALLY DO ANYTHING I WANT TO!!!

6/8/81

Early this morning off to Luxembourg, an amazing many-leveled city. No one sight is too amazing, but the whole picture is dramatic: bridges, airplanes, crumbling castles and underground caves, a park in a gorge, spires, overpasses, a canal or a river, below some ancient-looking shacks, square farm plots with people bent over their dry soil. A woman named Chris and I saw all this.

6/12/81 Reims

Last night I became terrified. I may be having nerve or psychological problems, but right now I'm too close to the situation to analyze it, and it doesn't make sense anyway, so I'll skip it for now.

6/19/81 Paris

For some reason my subconscious is on a guilt trip, or a repre-mandation [sic] trip anyway. That's the little beastly voice which is constantly inquiring about whether or not I'm making the most of whatever moment I happen to be living. Perhaps my subconscious is responsible for the heaviness and melencholy [sic] I so often feel hanging on me when I wake up, as well. It's like some ghastly, dripping garment that I have to peel from my body. Once I've wriggled free of it I feel light as smoke—elated.

6/22/81 Paris

I'll have to always remember the Cave, that perfect restaurant crowded with thick red candles that smelled faintly of flowers, the beautiful waiter and the piano player, whose music seemed to fall like snowflakes on the room. And also the two Lebanese students we* met later that night and had coffee with, the one so serious and honest, and looking like a statue off the side of a cathedral, with his dark beard and large eyes.

6/25/81 Chamonix

Today we† took trams up into the snow; what a totally different, awesome‡ world it was. Fog descending in loose tufts, mountains just seeming to leap into the air in sharp points—I can't believe I scram-

---

* My companion in Paris was a marvelous woman named Janet. She was a few years older, a ski instructor from Colorado who had ridden her bicycle from Belgium right into Paris, and who seemed capable of anything. In her company, I felt safe from the Terror, as I'd come to think of it.

† In Chamonix I had the good fortune to meet another travel companion: a college student at Chapel Hill named Sabra. We stuck together for a week or so, exploring Albi and Arles, and I felt protected by her presence.

‡ In 1981, there was not even a hint that "awesome" would achieve the colloquial ubiquity it has since attained. Then, it was a rare and genuine superlative, along the lines of "momentous" or "stunning."

bled around in the snow today in worn-out tennis shoes! We never reached Lac Blanc, but we had a helluva good time trying.

6/26/81 Albi

I feel an undercurrent of sadness running through my life, and I'm at a loss to understand it. Of course I'm so buoyant at times, and I do feel overjoyed and inspired and all that, but the sadness, the dull sense of fear (possibly more a fear of what isn't there than what is) seems always to resurface. When I feel <u>myself</u> not allowing <u>myself</u> to make the most of things, I fall into a pit of knowing despair; I know that I'm the only one who can judge the success and worth of my life, I know that my sad, empty feeling is a waste of my advantages, and I know that the only cause of that sad, empty feeling is myself. It's a circle that I'm drawing, yet I feel trapped inside it.

We decided to sleep by the river. Well, it rained. We fled to the train station at 4:00 am; wet, dirty, grumpy, yet still partially magnetized by the sight of the illuminated orange church against the purple-blue night.

6/27/81 Arles

We bought chicken, apples, yoghurt, cheese, wine, juice, whole wheat bread, and gorged overlooking the square and watching a haze of raindrops descend on the trees and tables. A off-key marching band paraded around and honked and slammed. From above we could see how wet their hair was.

6/29/81 train from Arles

Night. Beers. Boys; Italian and English. Wine, talk. Trouble. Sleep.

7/6/81 Rome

The question is this; do I treat my vague, shapeless whirlpool of fear that my life has not been "real"; ie has not, and will not

oh, I can't write about it. My mind moves too quickly. Forget it.

I feel like a doctor who snatches up his patient's heart monitor reading and realizes that he's been dead for the past 18 years without the doctor's knowledge. Why must I direct my obvious mental zeal into the destrutive channel of self flagellation? Too many questions, and I can't stop them. Once I come to a point when I could stop them, they already exist. I have that nervous, pursued feeling. I am definitely hiding from something. I run and run but its still the same.

Let's hope I can write about this later, because I can't see any other justification for it. And it had better be a masterpiece.[*]

---

[*] Clearly, the moment—if there was a moment—had already occurred. Maybe, like the Terror itself, it was too big and amorphous to capture. Maybe I knew it gradually, not suddenly. Maybe my dread of spending the rest of my life in a mental institution overshadowed whatever epiphany I'd had about what I might do with my life if by some fluke I managed to avoid the mental institution.

I did make good on my hope of writing about the experience. In my first novel, The Invisible Circus, the eighteen-year-old protagonist, Phoebe, follows much of my own itinerary through Europe as she tries to solve the mystery of her older sister's suicide. In Paris, Phoebe takes LSD, and I unleash upon her a version of the hallucinatory terror I'd felt.

Not a masterpiece, but a start.

E-3: October 25, 1986

Molly Lawless

RF	D. STRAWBERRY											
3B	R. KNIGHT											
LF	M. WILSON											
SS	R. SANTANA											

October 25th, 1986
BY Molly Lawless
E-3 "error, 1st baseman"

THE YEAR WAS 1986, AND I WAS IN **LOVE**.

ME, AGE 11

?

UNFORTUNATELY FOR ME, THE OBJECT OF MY AFFECTION WAS THE BOSTON RED SOX.

MY DAD INTRODUCED ME TO BASEBALL, AND WATCHING GAMES WITH HIM WAS ALWAYS LOTS OF FUN. BUT HE TOOK HIS DUTY SERIOUSLY. ONCE IT BECAME CLEAR THAT HE'D PASSED THE DEFECTIVE "RED SOX GENE" TO THE NEXT GENERATION, HE REALIZED HE'D HAVE TO GIVE ME **THE TALK**.

WHAT HAVE I DONE?

DO YOU THINK WE COULD WIN THE **WORLD SERIES** THIS YEAR?

THEY MAY GET REALLY CLOSE, BUT JUST WHEN YOU THINK THEY'RE FINALLY GONNA DO IT, ...THEY'LL SCREW IT UP.

BUT... WHY?

THAT'S JUST THE WAY IT IS.

BUT IT WAS TOO LATE. LIKE NEARLY SEVEN DECADES OF SOX FANS BEFORE ME, I HAD FALLEN VICTIM TO THAT MOST CLICHED OF DELUSIONS...

THIS IS THE **YEAR!**

1919   1986

A PROUD TRADITION

AND IT LOOKED LIKE IT MIGHT JUST BE. I WAS UNSURPRISED.

I'M SURE THEY DID THEIR BEST!

THEY'RE **BUMS!**

HMPH.

THE CHARMS OF LOCAL SPORTS RADIO

IN MY NAIVETE, NO MATTER HOW BADLY THEY'D SLUMPED, I NEVER DOUBTED THEM.

THE LAST TIME THE SOX MADE IT TO THE WORLD SERIES, IT WAS 1975. I WAS A MONTH OLD, AND LEGEND HAD IT THAT MY DAD WOKE ME UP CHEERING FOR CARLTON FISK'S FAMOUS "WAVED FAIR" HOMER.

YES! YES! WOO HOOO!

WAAA AAAAHH

DAMMIT, JIMMY!

THEY EVENTUALLY LOST THAT SERIES... OF COURSE.

AND NOW, ALMOST EXACTLY ELEVEN YEARS LATER, MY FATHER AND I SAT TOGETHER WATCHING OUR BOYS INCH EVER CLOSER TO A WORLD SERIES VICTORY — THEIR FIRST SINCE 1918! — OVER THE METS. IT WAS GAME SIX, AND THE RED SOX LED THE SERIES, 3-2. THEY JUST NEEDED TO WIN THIS GAME.....

...ONE LAST OUT...

...ONE STRIKE AWAY...

AND THEN IT HAPPENED.

AN EASY GROUNDER TO OUR FIRST BASEMAN...WHICH WENT **RIGHT THROUGH HIS LEGS.**

THE GAME WAS **LOST**. THERE WAS A GAME SEVEN, TOO... BUT THE TEAM, AS DEMORALIZED AS THEIR FANS, ENDED UP LOSING THAT, TOO.

EVERYTHING FELT DIFFERENT AFTER THAT. THE UNIVERSE HAD LET US DOWN. WAS IT POSSIBLE THAT LIFE... **WASN'T FAIR?**

THAT THERE WAS NO CONNECTION BETWEEN HOW BADLY YOU WANTED SOMETHING AND WHETHER YOU GOT IT?

I HAD NEVER WANTED ANYTHING SO MUCH... AND AS A RESULT, I HAD NEVER BEEN SO SPECTACULARLY DISAPPOINTED.

ARE YOU OKAY?

NO.

WHEN THE RED SOX FINALLY WON THE WORLD SERIES IN 2004, I WAS HAPPY, OF COURSE. AT THE SAME TIME, IT FELT UTTERLY **ANTICLIMACTIC.**

DAD!

CAN YOU BELIEVE IT?!

HONK! HONK

WOOO HOOO

YEAHHH

HONK HONK

IN 1986, I BELIEVED WE WERE ABOUT TO WITNESS A MIRACLE. BY 2004, I'D GROWN UP... AND KNEW THEY DIDN'T EXIST.

Landing

Paul Miller

It's not every day that you land in the middle of an earthquake.

I fly a lot, and I'm always in the suspended place between movement and stillness when the plane lands. It's a place in which I've become comfortable. One of the first things that goes through your mind is a sense of relief when the wheels touch the ground.

This didn't happen on Tuesday, August 10, 2010, after a five-hour flight from New Zealand to Port Villa, the capital of Vanuatu, part of an eighty-three-island archipelago in the middle of the South Pacific's "Ring of Fire"—a region of the world where several tectonic plates meet.

When we landed, the Richter scale measured 7.5, causing the ground and the plane to enter a complex dance. The plane's body trembled, creating frisson that sent shockwaves through my body. Everything suspends in an earthquake—time becomes elastic, electricity turns on and off, and all aspects of modern life grind to an eerie halt. No one on the Air Vanuatu Flight NF 0053 stood up. An announcement played over the speakers, telling us that our flight had landed in the middle of a highly irregular situation.

In the distance police sounded sirens to inform people to abandon homes and to get out into the open. We were stuck on the plane because the airport was considered unsound. The ground moved, and moved again. The plane rested on the tarmac, and we watched the airport sway with the ground tremors that rippled beneath our feet. Our captain said that the Pacific Tsunami Warning Center had announced that a twenty-three-centimeter tsunami had struck Port Vila. He warned us that bigger waves had been reported in other areas. Thousands of anxious people were running for the island's hills. As I sat in the plane with the world rippling around me, the South Pacific did a graceful ballet with all the aspects of civilization that I took for granted: the buildings swaying with the palm trees, the plane ebbing-flowing on the runway, and the water near the airport rippling with a power far beyond the ordinary movement of the waves.

That's when I really felt the metaphor of the moment. I was like a leaf in a pond, moving to the rhythms of the planet. Suspended, floating on the ocean of the earth, the logic of our civilization turned to flotsam and jetsam. The airport, the plane, the runway, all spoke a language that the earthquake didn't. Neither did I, but I could enjoy the beat.

The Verdict

Byron Case

I have to take the reporter's word, since I wasn't there. It's true that I was *physically* present—the slight twenty-three-year-old, dark hair, pale skin, seated at the defense table, dressed as if he were going to a funeral. That was seen to by the bailiffs, who brought me from my cell each day of the three-day trial. But some essential part of me fled my conscious body when the twelve strangers of the jury handed up the decision. I just couldn't handle the stress.

Even as nerve-wracking as those three days were, I found myself wishing for even more time. Locked away in the dank county jail with nothing to do but listen to card-playing thugs turn spades into a full-contact sport, it was months before the public defender's office sent my court-appointed lawyer. It took even longer to get the case's discovery, which finally let me piece together what had gone so terrifyingly wrong. On each revisiting of those twelve hundred pages of interviews and reports, I found something else to discredit the case against me. Of course there could never be enough time for that. I would never be satisfied with the number of holes I could poke in the state's arguments. I was determined to prove they had the wrong man—that I didn't murder my friend.

I've heard that a person brought to trial, even with a solid alibi and evidence supporting their claim of innocence, stands a 40 percent chance of being found guilty. Simply being seated on the wrong side of the courtroom is enough to put you away. It's practically a coin toss.

Listening to testimony and watching the prosecutors ham it up, I was unaware of the 40 percent theory. As a death penalty opponent and human rights advocate, however, I was far from naïve: I knew the system was riddled with imperfections. A life had been taken; someone had to be brought to account. Still, I had faith in the human capacity for reason. I held tightly to my belief that the jury would see the truth, in spite of the blanket of suspicion the prosecution set over them. To say I wasn't nervous would be a lie—there is always a measure of doubt—but I was not frightened.

Three days, then the parties rested and the jury was given the case. I was sent to a small holding cell that reeked of stale urine, down in the basement of the courthouse, to wait out the deliberation. Pacing, rocking, having calming conversations with myself, fighting down the compelling desire to vomit up my meager lunch. The jury could take days. Reconstructing on paper each witness's timeline of events had taken *me* nine hours. I was prepared to wait as long as it took, if it meant walking free into the arms of my friends and family who crowded the gallery.

Not four hours later, I was led back upstairs. My leg clicked with each step, thanks to the chafing metal brace that ensured I wouldn't run away. Not that there was anywhere to go.

My lawyer wrung his hands together as everyone filed into the courtroom once more. My whole life together in one room—it fanned the prickly flame of anxiety licking up my spine to see concentrated in that space everyone I stood to lose. There was my uncle, in from Maryland, offering a reassuring smile. There was my ex-girlfriend, trying her darnedest to look encouraging. There was my old roommate, giving a little wave. There was my friend and racing buddy, lips pursed and fingers crossed. There was my mother, eyes reddened from fearful tears. There were my grandparents. There was my former neighbor. There was the judge. There were the jurors.

"Be seated." And we were.

There was the foreperson, standing. There were the verdict papers.

"The defendant will rise." And I did.

Afterward, curled hopeless on the thin tarpaulin mattress of my cinderblock cell, there would be time to replay the moment my veins flushed with ice and my ears rang with my mother's single plangent yelp from behind me. There would be time to tearlessly grieve for myself weeping being only for those with a little strength left in them. There would be time to think and rethink. But only afterward.

One of the newspaper stories said that I winced. I have to take the reporter's word, since I wasn't there.

Nine Lives

Peter Kuper

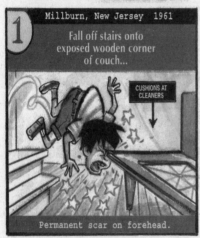

1 Millburn, New Jersey 1961

Fall off stairs onto exposed wooden corner of couch...

CUSHIONS AT CLEANERS

Permanent scar on forehead.

2 Cleveland, Ohio 1964

Game: Ride bike under playground chin-up bar, grab bar, let bike crash. Miss bar...

CRASH!

Knocked unconscious. Brain damage?

3 Negev Desert, Israel 1969

Climbing around looking in caves hoping to find additional Dead Sea scrolls. Find rock slide, almost meet God...

mommy!

Minor scrapes, major heart attack.

4 South Bronx, New York 1972

Buy LSD from dealer couple who are already tripping. Take lift from them, wind up in South Bronx...

W-WHERE DID YOU SAY YOU WERE GOING?

Still not sure what happened.

5 Manhattan, New York 1981

Drunk, stoned, climb out onto ledge of four story building. Admire view, teeter, try to hail cab...

Too stupid to die.

6 Puerto Escondido, Mexico 1983

Though warned about undertow, get stoned and swim anyway. Experience power of ocean, weakness of humans...

Lose pride, almost lose swim suit, life.

7 Koh Samui, Thailand 1989

Rent motorcycle (without helmet), take "magic mushrooms." Pause on one lane road, prepare to pull over when even bigger idiot passes going 60 MPH....

Bike sways, mushroom high ends.

8 Irian Jaya, New Guinea 1995

Trekking in remote region led by "guide" who steals supplies, extorts money and turns villagers against me...

Last visit to New Guinea.

9 Planet Earth, Solar System 20--

One never knows, do one?

KUPER

My Front Line

Jessica Lutz

'm sitting on the sofa with the man I love. He takes my hands and says, "I want to have a child with you."

The smile freezes on my face. My first impulse is to pull my hands out of his, but I keep them there. I want a future with this man. We're both high-performance journalists, zipping around the Middle East. We dive into war zones and adventure; we are part of the pack; we feel relevant, alive, important, and above all, we are addicted to high-octane surges of adrenaline in our veins. Does he really want me to give all that up?

"Well," I say, clearing my throat. "I don't believe in having a child and handing it over to a nanny. I think a child deserves a parent at home."

"Me too," he says. "I think you'd be such a wonderful mother." Does he know that I dumped the last boyfriend who said this to me? I was twenty then. Now I'm thirty-seven. But still.

"You can't seriously want me to sit at home with an infant while you have all the fun? To stop earning my own living and become dependent on you?"

He beams a smile at me. "You can trust me. I'll support you with everything I have."

"That's what you say. I can't risk not taking care of myself. You must be out of your mind."

Yet it's not long before I apprehensively agree and stomp off to the hospital to see my gynecologist. Fists in my pockets, scowl on my brow, and ignoring the sunshine, I mutter to myself all the way there.

> ## "It finally sinks in that simply risking my life does not make my life meaningful."

Why, oh why, have I not learned to say no? Especially to a man with deep blue eyes that make me feel as if I can spread my wings and float up into the vast space of the sky? *Why, why, why?* my footsteps rap.

And there I am, helplessly sprawled out in front of the doctor, who, with a nasty jerk, pulls out my IUD. "You'll be fine," she says at my contorted face, and pats my knees that dangle in the braces of the examination table. In the hospital café afterwards, I sip tea. I want to be alone with my big decision. What have I done? Am *I* not the one who's out of her mind? Well, I'm not going to eat healthier, drink less, or . . . or . . . hell, I'm not going to make love to him anymore.

Turns out that making love does not always make babies. I fight the temptation to force fate's hand with artificial help. Three years go by and I feel increasingly a failure—in my work, as a woman. And then, finally, I am pregnant. Together we go to the gynecologist again. "You're quite old," she observes. "Are you sure you want this baby?"

I could bite her head off.

Five months into my pregnancy, I am in Baghdad. The air is thick with the menace of the American invasion that can happen at any moment, with bombs that very soon will be targeted at the foreigners in town. All I want to do is put my arms around my precious belly. It finally sinks in that simply risking my life does not make my life meaningful.

My little daughter is seven now, and she has made me listen to my heart. Her presence has made me look in the mirror, confront some difficult issues, make more tough decisions. To my surprise I feel grounded, not stranded by motherhood.

And perhaps the most astonishing thing of all is to discover that an embrace by those little arms of hers, her wonky smile, can thrill me just as much as, if not more than, the triumph of surviving a burst of gunfire at any old front line.

Instructions

Julie Metz

My mom was the force of nature that ran our family until her death. She worked a full-time job; she paid the bills and prepared tax forms; she cooked meals both simple and ambitious. She knew where to buy good shoes on sale and how to get stains out of anything. She ironed my dad's pocket handkerchiefs. If my brother or I needed money for a school trip, she opened her wallet, a crack. Whether you wanted it or not, she always had opinions and advice, increasingly unwelcome as I passed from childhood into adolescence. I understand her frustrating predicament now that I too am the mother of a teenaged daughter.

When she was diagnosed in 2005 with mesothelioma, a terminal lung cancer, she began teaching my dad how to manage the myriad tasks that would make his future life without her possible: balancing a checkbook, cooking a meal, doing the laundry. I had the feeling that she was in a race against an unknown but imminent deadline to transfer all the information she had stored in her head. She gave me several recipes during this time that I treasure.

I saw her alive for the last time the day before she died. She could no longer speak, so our final conversation was (for the first time) one-sided. When I asked her if she was worried about leaving, she nodded yes. I told her that my brother and I would take care of our dad, that she shouldn't worry. I told her that there was nothing left for her to do, that we could handle everything. It was time to go. She waited until the following evening to leave, when we were all out of the house, with only the full-time nurse present. The nurse told us this happens a lot.

Some weeks after my mom died, my dad showed me a small piece of paper. I recognized the quavery handwriting on it as my mother's, much altered by her illness. This was the last thing she wrote, he told me, the instructions for fertilizing the roses in their weekend house garden. It was autumn when she died, the roses long dormant. In those long bedridden hours of her last weeks, she must have imagined them flowering again in the spring, knowing she wouldn't see them bloom, but that someone would.

It was somehow in that moment of reading her last instruction that I really knew my mother was gone.

2.10.01

Julia Halprin Jackson

Every year it's a bit different.

The first year, it was tragic. Every detail of February 10 was etched so clearly in my mind: the hard calluses on my palms from rowing competitions, the uncanny thirst in the back of my throat, that sinking feeling that I'd be doomed to adolescence forever. There were details that I'd attributed as somehow significant: the tulip painting on the hospital wall, the blue lights of the Tower Theatre mirroring the scene from the Sacramento River, the haunting chords of a Dave Matthews song. Everything is epic at sixteen years old. What boys think is important. What teachers say could influence career choices. And what a body feels like—there are few things that dictate puberty more than the clash of control and instinct.

The second year, the memory was no less vivid. The illusion of control followed me to a more adult life—my freshman year of college. I circled the lagoon that day, watching the gulls hem the coastline, realizing with a sudden finality that growing up meant taking ownership of imperfect organs.

> **There are so few moments of perfect drama in our lives—of actual, novel-worthy frustration—unembellished, random crises of faith."**

Every year it changes. Those first three years, February seemed so mournful. I wrote poems to cells. I was still angry. I explained everything all the time to anyone who so much as blinked in my direction.

The fourth year I was abroad. That was the year I decided an anniversary didn't have to be sad. We landed on Tenerife, in the Canary Islands, at midnight, and the minute it was February 10, I felt something new: defiance, in the form of optimism. And then I got dressed for Carnaval and learned how to relax in Spanish.

This tenth year, February 10 means something entirely different. February 10 is pancreas day, Julia day, adulthood day. I feel extraordinarily lucky. Not everyone can pinpoint the loss of idealism to one specific day. There are so few moments of perfect drama in our lives—of actual, novel-worthy frustration—unembellished, random crises of faith. For so many people, personal tragedy is not something so easily calculated: How does one quantify depression? Or the injustice of homophobia? Of lost opportunity to some invisible, imperfect law of human nature?

Mine is an unfairness I can chart, plot, and review. Mine is a plague of minimal pain. Mine is never a solitary journey. Mine is the confusion that actual life plots for all of us—the rearrangement of meals, the reminder that nobody is invincible, that there are consequences to every decision. Diabetes has always been a lesson in opportunity cost and effect, and while I never really appreciated my high school economics class, these things are more easily understood when one measures them in the form of a finger prick.

Ten years later, I no longer wonder who I'd be without diabetes. I'd be someone else, with some other Trojan horse, accomplishing other things. It doesn't matter. I am who I am just as a tree is just a tree, and a dog is just a dog. There is comfort to be found in identifying as something or someone. I am a diabetic, but I am also a woman, and a professional, a friend, a daughter, a sister, a person with opinions and aspirations. And, at times, catapulting blood sugar.

February 10. I look forward to the year when there are even more important anniversaries than this one.

The Bloodless Coup

Deborah Copaken Kogan

My teenage daughter showed up to my orthodox Jewish father-in-law's funeral in a striped miniskirt and a pair of shit-kicker boots. It couldn't be helped. The black dress I'd bought her two years earlier as my young father lay dying no longer fit, while Maurice, my ninety-five-year-old father-in-law, was here one minute, gone the next, which left no time to shop.

Jews being Jews, especially orthodox Jews being orthodox Jews, Maurice's body had to be buried within twenty-four hours, in a plot he'd reserved from a sect called Moriah, pronounced as in "How do you solve a problem like . . . ?": an apt question for this story. The Moriah used to run an orthodox shul on Manhattan's Upper West Side just above Zabar's, which my father-in-law joined after a decade spent hiding from Nazis. He purchased the plot soon after arriving in America because while Hitler was dead, you never knew with Nazis.

Hours after Maurice took his final breath, a Moriah representative contacted my mother-in-law to remind her that women, as per their misinterpretation of Halachic law, would not be allowed at the gravesite. This was not wholly unexpected news to the grieving widow, but it was also, under the circumstances, not the most welcome news either. Her current rabbi—who, like the majority of Jews, even the most orthodox, believes that shoveling dirt onto the deceased provides a necessary first step in the mourning process—was called upon to try to broker a better deal. The negotiations between the two sides lasted well into the night, at which point the Moriah rabbi finally broke down and agreed that the female mourners could accompany the body to the cemetery, so long as we remained hidden in the cars until the grave was three-quarters filled. I was told it had something to do with the possibility of contaminating the corpse with menstrual blood, although try as I might, I was unable to form a mental image of how such a defiling would occur without imagining scenes better suited to fetish porn.

The next morning, during the ride from the funeral home to the cemetery, I was sitting in the back seat with my two older children when I realized that I'd neglected to inform them of the whole girls-have-to-hide-in-the-car-until-the-grave's-three-quarters-full deal. So I told them.

"What are we, in the *stone age*?" said my fifteen-year-old son.

My daughter could barely speak, the look on her face hovering somewhere between disbelief and the kind of rage for which animal tranquilizers were invented. Then it hit me: Here was a girl, or rather a woman, by Jewish law, who had never, in her thirteen years, rubbed up against the absurdities of sexism. She'd never been told, as my mother once had, that only the boys in the family could go to medical school. Her right to vote has always been sacrosanct. Her school cannot claim they have no money for girls' sports. "But that's ridiculous!" she said.

"I know it is, sweetie," I said, "but that's the deal that was struck, so we have to stick to it."

At the cemetery, framed through the window of our car, a waddle of black-suited men encircled my father-in-law's grave, first rocking back and forth in prayer then doing the hard manual labor of burial. I tried to distract my daughter from her anger with stories about her grandfather. "Remember the time you were five, and he asked you what your favorite sandwich was, and you said, 'Proscuitto and brie?' and then Bonmaman said, 'That's not kosher,' and you said, 'What's kosher?'"

My mother-in-law reminisced about the morning, two decades earlier, when Maurice had belted out "The Marseillaise" while being wheeled down the hallway for the surgery no one thought he'd survive. My sister-in-law told stories of her father's imprisonment in plain sight during the Holocaust, how he learned to take communion and say, "Bless me father, for I have sinned," without sounding like an imposter. I wondered if anyone else in that car noticed the irony of our own imprisonment, sixty years later, in the back of that car. How complacently we wore the armbands of our gender without ripping them to shreds.

Finally, from our hidden vantage point, the grave appeared to be three-fourths full (give or take a sixteenth), so we women—about forty of us, many in the modest long skirts and post-matrimonial head-coverings typical of orthodox women—stepped out of the car and started walking toward the mound of earth. Which was when the black-hatted, white-bearded rabbi appeared, seemingly out of nowhere.

"What are you doing?" shouted the rabbi, now running toward us, shooing us back in the car, physically blocking all those uteri from getting any nearer to the grave. "This is a disgrace! Get back in the car! Back in the car!" Clearly, no one had told him about the deal. My mother-in-law started to cry. The other women were shocked into silence.

Which is when my daughter, all miniskirted 4'10" of her, clomped up to the rabbi in her boots and said, "Excuse me, sir, but my grandmother would like to bury her husband. We had a deal. Now, please, move out of my way."

Without looking back, she pushed her way past the rabbi and marched those boots straight toward the mound of dirt, where she yanked the shovel out of my husband's hand and thrust it deep into the earth. The rest of us women stood there, immobilized, not knowing how to proceed. Little Norma Rae could possibly be forgiven. Yes, she was thirteen, but she looked no older than ten. Her uterus, one presumed—or at least one presumed the rabbi was presuming—wasn't yet shedding its lining. "Come on!" she shouted, urging us on with her hand.

The rabbi from the cemetery stood his ground. "This is a disgrace!" he kept saying. "Get back in the cars!"

My daughter leaned on the shovel, her tiny frame dwarfed by it.

Seeing her standing there, armed for battle amidst that sea of black, I took my mother-in-law's hand in mine, and we made a wide detour around the rabbi. My sisters-in-law followed. A few seconds later, the entire amoeba of long-skirted women meandered its way toward the grave where, our bloodless coup thus complete, we grabbed some shovels and started digging.

Crying for Their Dog

Richard Ferguson

I was fourteen—a confused puberty stew of zits, girl craziness, cracking voice, and crippling shyness. It was summer. My family and I were vacationing in a small Wisconsin town. My dad had driven me to a swimming area across the lake from our cabin. He'd pick me up in two hours. Said I should stay put—swim, girl watch. Not to walk the three-mile stretch of lonely country road back home. I agreed. But after less than an hour, I'd had my fill of the murky brown water and the locals that looked straight out of *Guns & Ammo* magazine.

I began the long walk back to the cabin.

I was barefoot. It was a scorching summer day—ninety degrees. The asphalt beneath my feet felt double, triple that temperature. Every step was like walking through Dante's sixth circle of Hell, less the heresy and flaming tombs. My mind grew delirious. Road mirages wavered all about. My sweat-drenched Rush T-shirt stuck to my skinny chest. My jean shorts—hand-me-downs a size too big—kept slipping down to reveal butt crack.

At one point, when I reached a rise in the road, I approached a house on the other side of the highway. Two small children—a boy

and a girl—were on the front lawn playing fetch with their small border terrier. Upon spotting me, the dog ran out into the lonely stretch
of road. He barked at me. The children grew frantic, yelled: "Lucky!
C'mere, Lucky!"

I, too, yelled at the dog, waved my arms about, tried scaring him
away. That only made him angrier. He drew closer. With every step,
his collar jingled. I decided to ignore him, kept walking. But Lucky
followed. *Jingle jingle.* I stepped into the highway, met him head on,
stomped a foot, hollered at him to scram. He stood his ground, kept
barking. I kept stomping. The children kept shouting. The dog and I,
we just stood there, unmoving, at that rise in the road.

That's when a truck appeared out of nowhere.

I lunged backwards. The dog stayed put. One moment he was
there. The next moment: gone. The truck kept going. The children
began crying hysterically. Crying for their dog. Crying for their
mother. I was crying too. Kept saying I was sorry. I was only trying
to help. Now their mother was crying too. I don't remember her hair
color. Or whether she was fat or skinny, tall or short. All I remember
was that she was wearing a flower-print dress. On any other day except that one I would've thought that that dress was so beautiful.

There were no more cars in sight. Just me in the middle of that
desolate stretch of road with mirages as far as the eye could see, and
that dead dog. Except you could no longer even recognize him as a
dog. Now he was just some furry, greasy bloodstain on the road.

I stood there looking at those kids and their mother, crazed with
sadness. Kept looking at that stain in the road. It was a moment when
I would have gladly traded my own life for another.

The Quest

Ramona Pringle

With each step that I took, I felt a rush of adrenaline. The forest was at once spectacular and horrifying: a lush, jewel-toned canopy of leaves and brambles, speckled with the glowing eyes of lurking predators. The further I got from the relative civilization of base camp, the more I was at the mercy of the monsters in this enemy territory.

As I moved deeper into the dense forest, in search of one last night-saber beast to slay, I could feel the chill of mounting danger. My heart was pounding and my breath was becoming shallow. . . . Which was strange, I realized, since it wasn't *really* me in the forest; it was my avatar. The fight-or-flight mix of panic and thrill felt real, but my journey was a virtual one: I was being initiated into the game of World of Warcraft; this was my first quest.

I hadn't planned on playing World of Warcraft. Oddly enough, I'd never really been a gamer, but I also wasn't new to the world of online games. I'd been researching gamer culture as the interactive producer for a journalistic work project, and I was fascinated by the profound *real life* relationships I saw being

formed in virtual worlds. In my career I'd reported from red carpets and rock concerts, but my first shoot at a massive gaming convention in California was easily the most intoxicating event I'd ever covered, a sea of avatars come to life, with people dressed in exquisite, intricate costumes. I was enthralled by the collective love of the game, people's deep bond with their avatars, and their dedication to the people they played with. Most of all, my mind was blown by the love stories, by couples holding hands and pushing baby carriages, having found each other inside of the game. Their stories sounded like fairytales, getting to know each other through epic quests and overcoming obstacles to be together. These gamers were finding their soul mates inside of the game, meanwhile all of my best friends—smart, beautiful, successful women—were struggling to find the right guy. With digital citizens spending three billion hours a week playing online games, I couldn't help but wonder if they might be onto something that the rest of us should know.

My curiosity was magnified by questions in my personal life. From our first date, my boyfriend had swept me off my feet and I'd been positive he was *The One*. He was handsome, smart, and doting. After eight days he'd all but proposed, but eight months into our relationship, our picture-perfect romance wasn't what it had seemed to be. He was older, divorced, and saw his past as a series of mistakes he didn't want to repeat. He was jaded. As we started looking at apartments and planning out a future together, it became very clear that everything that made me excited made him nervous. I was crazy in love (or at least crazy about being in love), so I persevered, hoping to recapture the magic of when we'd first met. But I wanted a partner in crime, and he wanted a dinner companion, and eventually our differences became unbearable.

It was hard to end things and walk away from a relationship I'd had such high hopes for, harder yet to figure out how I'd let myself be so fooled. If it wasn't him, what was it that I wanted, or needed, from a partner? I set out to find answers—about life and love—and while some people turn to God or therapy or books, I decided to turn to video games.

So, I signed up for World of Warcraft and created my avatar, Tristanova. I opted to be a healer, rather than a hunter; my journey, after all, was about meaning rather than might, and Tristanova has the power to heal wounds and restore strength. Nonetheless, my first quest was to "kill four night-sabers."

Kill?

I specifically signed up to play a healer to avoid hunting. Should I stop playing, in protest of the hunt? No, I couldn't stop, not before I'd even begun.

It was eye for an eye, and I quickly learned that if I wanted to survive I had to play by the rules, even if they didn't match up with my modern sensibilities. I found that last night-saber and completed my first quest. It was a bittersweet beginning; I'll be honest, I whispered a little mourner's prayer for the creature.

I was exhausted. My strength was low, and my health was dwindling. It was too much to continue on alone. I decided that if I was going to keep playing, I needed a partner, and so after that first quest I found Caethis, a world-class game designer and veteran gamer who offered to be my guide as I ventured further into online worlds.

Although we lived in different cities, when we logged into the game together, the distance between Caethis and I disappeared; in the game, we were together on a mission, side by side. I would catch myself being conscious of how close our avatars were standing to each other, surprisingly aware of how real it felt. His avatar would protect me, shield me from harm, and in return I would use my powers to keep him strong and heal him after battle. Our relationship became symbiotic. Despite the fact that it was all data and pixels, I felt safe and I felt needed. I'd never actually met Caethis, but I quickly found myself developing a crush on him.

I spent my nights in World of Warcraft; two, three, four hours would just pass, and after eight weeks of logging in practically every day, I began to realize that what Tristanova needed to survive in virtual space was exactly what I had been missing in my relationship. I needed someone to balance my strengths and weaknesses. Just as Tristanova flourished playing alongside a Warrior, I needed someone in the real world who would be there when night-sabers needed to be slain. I thought about all the things I'd been looking for: excitement, romance, passion, intellect. Now, I found myself longing for something else: a partner. Someone to be at my side throughout life's adventures. Someone to protect me. Someone who could count on me to protect him in return.

I knew now it was time to resume my quest in the real world.

I was crazy in love (or at least crazy about being in love), so I persevered, hoping to recapture the magic of when we'd first met. But I wanted a partner in crime, and he wanted a dinner companion, and eventually our differences became unbearable.

Early Dismissal

Robin Wasserman

When you're a rational, clear-eyed, culturally conversant, healthy, mature, and stable grown-up, there are certain fundamental facts you know about the world. One of which is that twelve-year-old girls come in only two varieties: the ones on the cusp of dumping their best friends and the ones who will be dumped. The corollary to this is that it would be rather inappropriate for any rational, clear-eyed, culturally conversant, healthy, mature, and stable grown-up to care. Much less still hold a grudge.

I was born to be a dumpee, the epitome of quiet and bookish, with oversized glasses stuck to my face since nursery school and an oversized helping of glee at any opportunity to be the teacher's pet. I was easily bored, easily charmed, and easily led, a ready-made sidekick to the school's resident (if relatively mild) wild child.

I was also, having been reared on a steady diet of *Anne of Green Gables*, well versed in the pursuit and cultivation of "kindred spirits," and desperate to get one of my own. Once I finally did, it was as if I morphed into a fifties cheerleader who'd just scored a varsity beau, obsessed with the trappings of my new status. Instead of letter jackets, fraternity pins, and promise rings, I coveted friend-ship bracelets, science project partnerships, manic sleepovers, and, above all, the best friend necklace, which could be broken in two and worn by each of us as a badge of our unbreakable bond. But the reasoning behind it all was the same. These were talismans: proof to the world that I was no longer an *I*, but a *we*.

Don't get me wrong. I liked my best friend well enough—just not as much as I liked having a best friend, *any* best friend. I was a fright-ened child, not to mention an only child, and my best friend was my security blanket, the universe's guarantee that I would not face the future alone. She was also my mirror—a far more flattering mirror than the one hanging on the back of my bedroom door. Her very exis-tence was evidence that I couldn't possibly be *that* ugly, *that* awkward, *that* unlovable, because she was perfect, and she not only loved me, but loved me *best*.

So you can imagine my surprise that sixth-grade day in the play-ground, when, lurking in corners as I was wont to do, I overheard her casually tell some new group of admirers that, no, I wasn't her best friend, why would anyone ever think that?

That was it. No dramatic breakup scene. No slammed books, no rumor mongering, no cafeteria shunning, no mean girl antics what-soever. Which was almost worse, because if I had become her worst enemy, it would at least have been an acknowledgment that I was once her best friend.

Instead, from that moment on, I was nothing.

It was the first time in my life it had occurred to me that kindred spirits might not last—that life, no matter how many talismans of at-tachment you accumulated, would be a constant struggle against be-ing alone. There would eventually, at least after I'd crossed the social desert of junior high, be other best friends. Better ones. But much as I may have believed in those friendships, I have never again taken it for granted that they would last. In the real world, the Grown-up world, people leave, people die—people sometimes just get bored and move on to another part of the playground. Anything can happen.

There are certain fundamental facts that twelve-year-old girls know, while grown-ups, even the wisest of us, have forgotten: the names of Magellan's ships, the difference between mitosis and meiosis, the formula to calculate the volume of a cube—and the fact that BFF is not meant to be ironic.

Knowing that no one's guaranteed to stick around has probably made me a better friend, and I'm certainly a better accessorizer now that I've left the ratty friendship bracelets and plastic necklaces behind.

But I'll admit: I liked believing in forever.

Burning Up

Qraig R. de Groot

Surrounded by a bumper crop of bright yellow dandelions during a late spring morning in 1983, I sat on the edge of my front lawn listening to the radio. Fiddling with its giant dial tuner, as a mishmash of music droned from one tiny speaker.

A few months past twelve and completing the last weeks of sixth grade, come September I'd be moving up to junior high. The thought sent fear and dread, jumbled with just a tinge of thrill, through my prepubescent body. At that moment, I was still a big man on the elementary school campus. My class had recently voted me "Mr. Congeniality," and I was narrating the sixth-grade play I helped write with Michelle, my best friend since age three. We posed the question, "What will the sixth-grade class of School 4 in Clifton be up to in twenty years?" Michelle fancied herself to be a top-notch teacher, while I saw myself as a rich, world-famous Dalmatian breeder.

Back in my Dalmatian-lacking life, I randomly scanned through radio stations, stopping for a moment at an aging disco tune, a current Top 40 hit, or an arena rock anthem. Nothing seemed to hold my interest for long. A catchy dance song caught my ear and I paused to enjoy the tail end. An unfamiliar tune followed. My fingers were ready to start turning the dial again. But before I could, she began to sing about being on fire.

I immediately snapped to attention and let go of the tuner. The simple lyrics over this strange rock-infused disco beat were electrifying.

I leapt to my feet. The song now had my full attention as the singer chirped on about quenching desires, pounding hearts, and being down on her knees!

Oh, do you wanna see me down on my knees
Or bending over backwards now, would you be pleased

Nothing had ever jumped off the radio before and basically beat me into submission. Goosebumps ravaged my skin as the singer's voice penetrated every single pleasure spot on my body. A mind-blowing chill went up my spine. I turned the volume up as loud as it would go. As the song ended—way too soon for my liking—the announcer revealed what it was.

The song was "Burning Up." The singer was Madonna. And she was about to change the soundtrack of my life.

Since then, Madonna has always been by my side. She got me through those first few awkward days of junior high and stayed with me during my painfully insecure high school years. When I went away to college, I cried to Madonna about my loneliness. Then, four years later I danced with her and my friends on graduation night.

Madonna was there for my first sexual experience with a woman, and then later with a man. It was she who gave me the confidence to reveal who I truly was. She always encouraged me to express myself.

She boldly moved with me from New Jersey to San Francisco, then tentatively to Los Angeles, and finally dejectedly back to the

East Coast. Madonna cheered me along while I ran my first marathon and comforted me when my father died.

With Madonna's guidance, from that first moment I heard her sing "Burning Up," I burgeoned from a timid boy into a confident man.

Six-Word School Moments from SMITH Teens

Lunch was spent kicking concrete walls.
—*Bailey A.*

I got a part. Fate sealed.
—*Natalie M.*

Skipped prom for Magic: The Gathering.
—*Codi P.*

People laugh at my Harvard dreams.
—*Emily G.*

Came out to everyone but parents.
—*Stephanie C.*

Least typical cheerleader you'll ever see.
                    —*Becca B.*

Lost my identity when I moved.
                    —*Kristen G.*

Band has saved
me from insanity.
                    — *Hannah R.*

**No
acceptance
letters
yet.
Freaking out.**
                    —*Matt R.*

*Class weirdo hearts class president.
            Doomed.*

                    —*Rebecca H.*

Maiden Days

Judy Collins

I was trained as a classical pianist, and until I was about fourteen I thought that's what I was going to do.

But one afternoon in 1954, I came home from school to practice and I heard a folk song on the radio: "The Gypsy Rover," sung by Elton Hayes. It was from a movie called *The Black Knight* with Alan Ladd, a story set in King Arthur's Camelot.

The song simply changed my life.

I heard this and ran and bought a copy of it, and I never looked back.

Part of the appeal was that it was a story about a girl who runs off from her father and joins up with a gypsy rover. I suppose it was the story of the Robin Hood of the time. It was real, and it had a lot of drama in it. This girl leaving her father's castle and running off into the woods—very, very dramatic.

I told my father that I had to have a guitar. He was thrilled and thought it was a great thing for me. He loved the music too, just loved it. I played the guitar and the piano for a long time—but when I was on the road I knew that wouldn't work with the folkies around. They weren't playing the piano.

In 1966 I made an album that had a lot of extremely difficult things on it—Bertolt Brecht, Jacques Brel, Leonard Cohen—and I had to bring the piano back into my life in a serious way. That's when I started writing songs. I knew I had to play the piano in order to write songs; I could no more write songs on the guitar than I could fly.

I had been learning the Rachmaninoff second piano concerto when I discovered folk music. I loved classical music, but these things happen and your life changes and there's hardly anything you can do about it. Before you know it, you're onstage with a guitar in your hand singing "Diamonds and Rust."

Just a Man

Nadja Cada

On my thirteenth birthday, my mother handed me a letter and said, "I wanted to wait till you were older to give you this, but I think it's time. This is a letter that your biological father wrote on the day you were born." I looked at her wide-eyed, took the envelope and opened it with care and caution. I began reading the thoughts of someone who, up to this point, had been just a man I never knew.

In tight, cursive handwriting he sang praises of love and pride for his beautiful new daughter. He said that everyone adored her and that she had captured his heart. He described her dark, full head of hair and deep gray eyes and the joy of knowing this was his daughter.

I finished the two-sided letter and looked to my mother. She was calm. "He really did love you," she said. At that moment I had questions. But the man who could answer them had been gone for twelve years.

Motherless

Tamara Pokrupa-Nahanni

My mother died when I was twelve. A couple of days before she passed, I asked her to record a translation of an English passage into Slavey, the language of our people. My sister went to her hospital bed to do the recording while I was at school. A couple of weeks later I sat down to listen to the tape. I recognized my mom's beautiful script writing on the label and was thankful that I would be

able to listen to her voice anytime I missed her. I pressed play, and no sound came out. I tried the whole tape. Nothing had been recorded. In the last few minutes of listening to that silent playback, I realized that I couldn't live in a fantasy where a voice recording replaced my mother, and the fact that she really was gone—that I was motherless—finally set in.

The Ripple Effect

Anthony Doerr

In the week after graduating from college in 1995, I went trout fishing with my dad. One day we were wading a cold, tea-colored river in western Maine called the Rapid, and the sun bounced off the water and cooked our faces as we fished, and by afternoon our bodies had reached that strange, subdivided place bodies reach when one half is sunk in icy water and the other half is broiling. My dad sat down on a big, midstream boulder whose top stood out of a steady, deep flow, and waved me over for lunch.

As I picked my way toward him, through waist-deep water, I stumbled and drove my kneecap into a submerged rock. My legs were a bit wooden from being in the river all day, so the pain was sneaky, an underwater pain, that came on slowly, and as it swelled and bloomed, it became harder to move in my waders. I didn't lose balance though, and I didn't mention it to Dad. I climbed up the rock, set down my rod, and watched my father put a handful of chips into his mouth.

And then my memory stops for a second.

That's not quite accurate. What I remember is something like a dream, a shimmering interval of blue, in which my eyes were open but there wasn't much to see, just a sense that I was being carried through a world composed entirely of different shades of blue, all flowing against one another. At the outer edge of that world someone was kicking distantly—a faraway, insistent drumming—but it was easy enough to ignore. I knew, in fact, that I would ignore it.

Who knows how long I was gone? A few seconds? A year? At some point I was jerked back into this world. My father's fist was on the front of my waders and he was squinting at me as if to say, "Did you just do that?"

I coughed water out of my nose. My baseball hat was gone. My knee hurt. My shirt was soaked and my waders were partially full of water. Apparently I had tipped backward off the rock and my whole upper body had gone under while my legs stayed up on the boulder.

> *"People die for ideas and countries and each other. I would have died for what? A few brook trout. Some corn chips and a sandwich."*

Dad said, "I thought you were cooling off your head."

I thought: *My dad just saved my life.*

Hours later, in a restaurant, at dusk, I thought: A life is something you think you're building, five thousand days, five million memories, all the classes I took in college, all the friends I'd made, and everything can get wiped out in a second? While you're wading across a pretty stream on a sunny day to eat Doritos with your dad?

People die for ideas and countries and each other. I would have died for what? A few brook trout. Some corn chips and a sandwich.

I went to the bathroom and looked in the mirror and thought: You aren't much.

Every few years since then certain memories reemerge, unbidden, like small points of light in the blue field of my past, rippling steadily into the present even as they recede farther away, sending their reverberations into the present, even as they intersect with the ripples from other moments: a night in the hospital on morphine, my wife's eyes fading beneath anesthesia, watching a doctor set my son's shattered arm. Live long enough and a life starts to look like an interference pattern of intense and total complexity, hundreds of memories rebounding, participating, and intersecting with one another.

In my own life, that one moment, sixteen years ago on the Rapid River, still sends its ripples into my hours. Your life is a rag, those ripples say. Your life is a shadow.

Sometimes you feel the power of your existence flare in you—through you—with so much intensity your knees buckle.

And yet a single misstep, some bad luck, a convergence of instants, and it's gone.

You aren't much. And yet you are everything.

Positively 93rd Street

Matthew Leader

I vaguely recall the lead-up to it all—a routine physical, the crusty old GP bopping my knee with a hammer, the two of us joking about me getting old at twenty-nine because of my sedentary Manhattan law job. And looking back I'm amazed that I didn't register the increasing urgency of the receptionist's messages telling me to come back in to discuss the results of my blood work. But back then I wasn't a health worrier, so it didn't strike me as important or strange, the two prerequisites for memory. There must have been that first big moment, when the doctor actually said "you tested positive" or "you have HIV," but I don't recall it. There was only the mundane cluelessness of before and the sickening haze of after. In the middle, at the exact center of impact, sits a little erasure that may never be filled in.

But it happened, and I recall the time immediately following that visit like a slideshow seen from the bottom of a well. Slow, dreamlike days flowing back and forth into terrified, wakeful nights. Halting calls to parents and ex-girlfriends. Then more calls, during the silent nights, to support-lines staffed by strangers, men who should have been dead long ago but now are kept alive through their daily drug cocktail. These men shared stories of how they too were sure it was a mistake. You need to accept it, they say. Because the odds of an actual mistake are vanishingly, heartbreakingly small. And then, after a week of this zombie life, the final slide.

And then the clock wound back. Monday morning, 8 a.m., on Broadway and 93rd Street. Standing in front of a deli, holding my briefcase and my cell phone, calling for the follow-up results. I remember the pause as the receptionist got the doctor on the line, and with bright, frozen clarity hearing the words: "There must have been a lab error. I'm sorry. Congratulations." And then hearing something angry in Korean as I collapsed and lay weeping in a sidewalk display of apples for a long, long time.

Of course, after a while, my life went back to normal. In the years since I have been sad, happy, fulfilled, disappointed. Like many, I struggle to be satisfied with life. And I suffer when my desire to be great, to stand out, is unrealized. But once in a while, I am graced with the perspective to remember that moment when the dynamite clock suddenly stopped ticking. How light and giddy and indescribably joyous I was to suddenly just be regular. And then, for a few seconds every week or month or year, everything that is fades in comparison to what might have been, and I achieve perfection.

Smack Talk

Melissa Febos

It's barely dark when the first guests begin to arrive. The Boston summer is hot, and my friends and I are young and restless, wound like springs. We are smart but not straight, wild but not crazy. We just want to get high, and not because we have a problem, but because it feels so good.

I hold a lighter underneath the foil, and watch the pink crystal meth powder bubble into liquid, releasing a thin stream of smoke. I suck up the smoke through a hollow Bic pen and hold that acrid breath in my chest for as long as I can. Barely a wisp comes out when I finally exhale, and the circle of boys around me claps.

Lex is high too. She drifts through the apartment in black leather pants and slicked-back hair. She still has the face of a doll, the same tiny mouth and enormous blue eyes that she had when we were kids. She wants to dress me up, she says. How come I never wear skirts? She leads me into her room and shuts the door. The room is spare, the noise outside muffled. I feel safe and removed. As high as I am, I can feel my love for her more precisely than ever before. It is like a seashell—sharp-edged on the outside but smooth as glass inside. It is engraved with our history: The prank calls we made, back when you could still get away with that; the summer she taught me how to shoplift and twist the hood ornaments off cars; the time she stole a pair of my mother's earrings, and I stole them back.

I am high enough to not hate my legs, and I let her dress me in a skirt. Gingerly, she draws on my eyelids with a soft pencil. Our noses are inches apart, and though my eyes are closed, I can feel her breath on my face. She leans back, appraising me, then leans back in with a mascara wand. She sneaks into Monie's room to steal a wig and a pair of patent leather stilettos—stripper shoes. She adjusts the blond bob on my head and nods approvingly. I practice walking, like a newborn calf, and she smiles at me, sweet and wry.

"I've always hated you," she says, and I stumble. "I mean, only as much as I loved you. But I guess that's kind of a lot."

Sitting on the edge of the bed, her legs are crossed. Her leather pants squeak as she bends to reach under the bed and pull out a mirror. On it is a small pile of dirty-looking powder. Holding the mirror in her lap, she uses her driver's license to separate a tiny mound of powder from the larger one. This she snorts with a rolled-up bill, leaning her head back and exhaling through her mouth. My hands are wet and cold. I wipe them on the back of my skirt.

"You were always the smaller one, so pretty and lucky, with your pretty, lucky family," she says. She rubs her nostril with vigor and rolls her eyes back. "I talked terrible shit," she says to the ceiling. "To all your friends, all the boys. It didn't make me feel better, but it didn't seem to hurt you either." Lowering her gaze, she looks me in the eyes. I can't do anything but look back. "I don't tell anyone what a slut you were because I like you better gay."

We stare at each other through our respective highs, and there is surprisingly little urgency in the air. I feel unsurprised. Slightly flattered even. But I am sad, and not because of what she has said. It

"She sneaks into Monie's room to steal a wig and a pair of patent leather stilettos—stripper shoes. She adjusts the blond bob on my head and nods approvingly. I practice walking, like a newborn calf, and she smiles at me, sweet and wry."

seems that I have always been this sad, that her words have simply pulled the lid off of it, let the sadness flood into me. The lid will close again, and in the meantime I start taking off the silly outfit.

"Don't!" Lex says. "I just wanted to see if you were still prettier than me." She sighs. "You are."

I love her again then and can feel the sharp edge of that seashell as if it is clenched in my fist.

"I love you," she says, as if reading my mind. "Sorry about the honesty. It's the smack talking."

Firecracker

Arthur Suydam

When I was five years old, a group of kids and I were out-side playing and got a hold of some fireworks that hadn't gone off. We'd seen a lot of cartoons where you tie a string to the dynamite, and the coyote is running with the dynamite in his pocket and it blows up. So we took some string and we tied it to one of the firecrackers that hadn't gone off, and then we got some matches, and then we tried to light the firecracker with the matches. A wind came by and blew the string against my clothes. My clothes caught on fire. I was burned on more than 50 percent of my body.

I was in the hospital for a year, wrapped up like a mummy from head to toe. They thought I was going to die. I had to learn to walk again a year later. From that moment on, I have always felt as if I lost a year out of my life. I grew up with kids who were one year younger than me. So I tried to make up for that lost year, physically and mentally. I developed a competitive nature.

When I was in the hospital that year, my parents brought me comic books. When I was released, I started drawing characters from the comic books. Fifteen years later, I was young adult. And I was a professional comic artist.

The Silver Harmonica

Andrew D. Scrimgeour

As Christmas approaches, my wife's relatives often talk about the follies of "nebbing" for the edification of the younger set—nebbing being a regional Pennsylvania term for sneaking about the house when grown-ups aren't around, checking drawers, cupboards, and crawl spaces for hidden gifts. While I have never been prone to nebbing, one year I did open a package well in advance of the twenty-fifth. But I didn't spy it tucked away on the top shelf of a closet. It found me. My brother Paul surprised me with an early gift—a brown leather jacket.

I asked if he would still gift wrap the coat and place it under the tree for rediscovery, for I didn't want it to miss his signature touch. Paul's gifts always looked as if they've been stolen from a Saks Fifth Avenue window display. If you walked into our living room and surveyed the gifts under the tree, you would have no difficulty spotting which were from him. They would be the elegant packages—the ones most likely to have been left by the Magi themselves.

My brother may be the most persnickety person I know when it comes to holiday wrap, but he is even better known for the exacting way that he chooses the gift itself. He would never buy a generic present for anyone; it must be something that declares that he knows a person well. His gifts are often unusual and require hours of planning, searching, and worrying. Consequently, you never find yourself later discreetly contributing his offering to the local thrift shop, church bazaar, or elephant gift exchange.

His most publicized offering was not a family gift but one he created in the early seventies for the citizens of northern California. He had learned of a cost-cutting decision to deck the toll plaza on the Golden Gate Bridge with plastic garland for the holidays. The thought of artificial greens marring the iconic structure was intolerable to Paul, but instead of merely grousing, he set out to remedy it. He contacted the Golden Gate Bridge Highway and Transportation District and persuaded the "Scrooge Party" bureaucrats to bless a counter-proposal: to properly adorn the entrance to the Bridge on the San Francisco side at his expense. The *San Francisco Examiner* saluted him for the handcrafted, regionally appropriate wreaths that soon greeted cars heading north over the golden span—redwood boughs studded with bows as vibrant as Paul's own red hair.

Many years later Paul and my parents came to Colorado to spend the holidays with my family. The master of gift-giving was uncertain about what to buy Mom, for she had suffered several strokes, was deep into Alzheimer's, and often didn't know us. She seemed content to sit in a cardigan sweater by the fireplace and watch the pageantry of the season—the decorating, wrapping, cooking, baking—unfold around her. The mom with whom we sat in the second pew of our dad's church and learned to read music by following her gossamer voice up and down the staffs in the hymnal, no longer sang, and rarely spoke.

So Paul was anxious as we opened gifts around the tree in the shy light of Christmas morning. When it came to be his turn to distribute gifts, he handed Mom a stylish package that suggested jewelry. With tedious care her fingers worked off the ribbon and wrap and lifted out a silver harmonica. She had played a mouth organ when she was younger, but had been without one for years. Dad said, "Why don't you play something, Sylvia?" I winced, thinking that he was putting too much pressure on her; but no, her eyes danced. Cautiously, she raised the slender harp to her lips, blew a few tentative chords, then— slowly, flawlessly—played "Jesus Loves Me." It was as if she had been practicing it for months, just for that occasion.

During December many people listen for church bells and familiar carols, but I, in my brown leather jacket, listen for the plaintive strains of a silver harmonica.

Denial

Kathy Ritchie

I was sitting at the kitchen table when I spotted a sample box containing the memory drug Aricept. I asked my mom why she was taking it. She told me that her doctor thought it might be a good idea since her memory was failing her. My first thought was of Ronald Reagan. He died of Alzheimer's disease, an incredibly long and drawn out process (from what I remembered). Could my mom have this disease? *No. Absolutely not. How could I cope with this? I can't change her diaper. I can't deal with this. I'm only twenty-seven.*

I don't remember feeling any profound sense of grief or loss—my own mother didn't seem too troubled that her doctor gave her a bunch of pills (beautifully packaged and marketed) for an incurable, brutal disease. I do, however, remember what I was wearing: a turquoise sweater with an oversized turtleneck and bell sleeves. My ex-fiancé hated it. It was the only thing that kept me warm. That is, until denial set in. It covered me like the thickest, coziest fleece blanket.

Denial is an awesome thing. It allows you to rationalize what you know deep down to be horrifyingly true. As I sat there, I started running through a list of all of her various peculiarities that had started springing up from nowhere—those subtle new behaviors that you make you think, *Oh Christ, could it be?*—and I explained away everything. Or more accurately, swept everything under the rug. *My mom doesn't have Alzheimer's disease. Mom just retired. Her increased forgetfulness, her inability to get my name right the first time ("David, Betsy, Anita, Vilma, KATHY!"), her mounting anxiety and abandonment of basic household chores is because she no longer has a routine or maybe she's a little homesick for her native Ecuador. It'll pass. She's fine.*

And those pills? Just another doctor peddling another drug.

Time drags in purgatory. It's been over six years since that moment in my mom's kitchen. We were recently told that she might only have two-to-three years to live—this, after learning she *isn't* dying from Alzheimer's disease. Her gray matter is turning to mush because of a lesser-known, more sinister kind of dementia: Frontotemporal dementia. A dementia that affects those areas of the brain that control personality, behavior, language—you know, those little things that make us who we are.

If you asked me today which "stage" of grief I currently inhabit, I couldn't answer—it goes beyond your typical seven. Most days, I just don't feel what I probably should feel.

Denial is always a good place to start. It coats your entire nervous system, temporarily shielding you from a grotesque reality, a Pepto-Bismol of the brain.

My moment of denial was the very first step in a long, dragged-out farewell party.

Mercy

Steve Anthony Leasure

I saw the stop sign just fifty feet ahead. I had taken my eyes off the unfamiliar road for just a few seconds.

That was all it took.

I said to myself, "I'm dead," as a tractor-trailer raced toward the same intersection at the same moment. I hit the brakes, knowing the collision was going to occur. It was going to happen and I was going to die. It was reality. My life was over. This was the end.

And yet I felt nothing but relief. God had finally released me. I was going to die and finally be free of all the guilt, fear, loathing, indecision, unspoken conversations—the incompleteness. The weight of being alone in the world, shy, romantic, suddenly lifted off my shoulders.

As clichéd as it may sound, in that single moment my life flashed before my eyes: A failed business. A wasted degree. A quiet, stuttering boy picked by the girls as most popular in his sixth-grade class.

I revisited my hometown, saw my sister's smile, felt my mother's hugs, ate my first Pop-Tart, heard my father's voice, and raced my brother across the backyard.

I felt sadness and joy, but mainly joy. All of the could've, should've, would've doubts didn't matter anymore.

My car skidded past the stop sign and into the intersection.

Awkward in high school. College at twenty. Graduation at thirty-five. Savannah. Atlanta. North Carolina. Tennessee. Susan. Jennifer. Terry. Lisa. Katherine. Carol. Tammy. The gentleness. Skin touching skin. But never an "I love you" that really took.

> **"The blood tasted like pennies in my mouth. Overhead the sky was cloudless. Lifeless. Godless. Meaningless. In a perverse way I was hoping I would have scars from this."**

The first time I wrote my ABCs. My Hank Aaron baseball cards. Nervous job interviews. Five-day-old beards. Sports trophies. Goof-ups. Daydreams. Brother, sister, mom, dad.

Then the collision. A fan of white light. The white room. The shattered glass. And the mercy.

I slammed into the side of the truck still going fifty miles per hour. The airbag opened. *Spin! Spin! Spin! Spin!* Four loud, angry rotations, as if the car were a toy top. The front hood compressed. My knees jammed into the dashboard, and I eventually came to a stop.

Someone opened the door and pulled me out. I stumbled across the hot asphalt and fell into a ditch. The world smelled like gasoline and honeysuckle.

The blood tasted like pennies in my mouth. Overhead the sky was cloudless. Lifeless. Godless. Meaningless. In a perverse way I was hoping I would have scars from this.

Several moments passed, and in the distance I could faintly hear a siren slowly growing louder.

I had remembered it all—every insult and every emotion. Every poem I had ever read or written I suddenly knew by heart. I remembered the beauty too—emerald eyes, soft sighs, thighs the color of tea with honey. I had seen everything—every moment, every face, every embrace. Everything but the presence of God.

As I felt the blood trickle down my neck, I finally understood. The best that you can expect is to survive, to struggle with the past, to build upon your own ruins and to pray that either God or the Devil will have mercy on you and that somewhere along the way you will find more love than you deserve.

The Hidden Dangers
of Blood Magic

Robert Joseph Levy

February 14, 1994. Harvard College: Cambridge, Massachusetts. The dining hall is done up for Valentine's Day. Pink and white crêpe paper overhead, scattered rose petals underfoot, a long credenza piled high with treacle—cupcake pyramids, red velvet cakes, lollipop trees, wicker cornucopias of candy hearts, all bearing holiday slogans of commitment and devotion.

"Be Mine." "Marry Me." "I Love You." "You're My Sweetie."

And of course, I've never felt so alone. I'm overheating with unhappiness, palms slick with sweat, smile held so tightly in place it might as well be Saran-Wrapped to my face. Laughter all around, from my roommate and his girlfriend and everyone else. But not here, not where I am. Not inside.

I reach for an object of sublimation: a plastic-encased lollipop bearing the single word "Magic." I can't get the wrapper off, though, not even between my gritted teeth, so I take up a kitchen knife from beside a cake plate and attack the candy's wrapper with a hard and swift stab of frustration. The knife slips and pierces the soft web of my hand; in a spray of bright crimson, I proceed to bleed across the table of sticky confections in an astonishingly powerful torrent. It takes half an hour and an entire roll of paper towels to quell.

One week later, I meet my first boyfriend. And then, he breaks my heart.

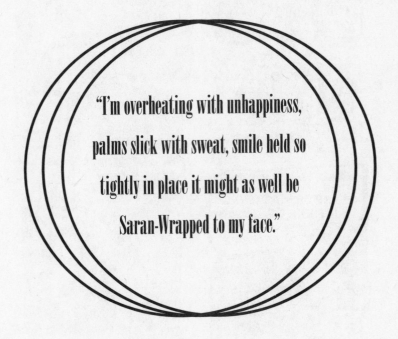

"I'm overheating with unhappiness, palms slick with sweat, smile held so tightly in place it might as well be Saran-Wrapped to my face."

Blogging Toward Oblivion

Emily Steinberg

YES, I ADMIT, NOT THE BRIGHTEST THING TO WRITE.

BUT, SOMETIMES THE TRUTH SQUEAKS OUT....

UNBIDDEN

NOW, HAD THIS TANTALIZING BIT OF HONESTY JUST BEEN LEFT ALONE DANGLING OUT IN THE BLOGOSPHERE,

ALL WOULD HAVE BEEN COPESETIC.

INSTEAD, I WAS OUTED BY A SASSY 13 YEAR OLD BOY WHO HATED ART CLASS.

HE GOOGLED ME AND FOUND MY BLOG!

THEN, HE TRIUMPHANTLY HANDED THE OFFENDING ENTRY OVER TO THE POWERS THAT BE.

THE PRINCIPAL AFFECTIONATELY KNOWN AS HELMET HEAD FOR HER UNBELIEVABLY UPTIGHT AND SHELLACKED HAIRDO, SUMMONED ME TO A DISCIPLINARY MEETING IN WHICH I WAS SUMMARILY RELIEVED OF MY DUTIES.

Tucked Away

Hope Rehak

I am twelve years old. It's September and my mom has told me to pack up my sleeping bag, which has been out since the summer camp days of July. But she and my dad can't stop watching television, which is so strange for them. They never watch television. It's scaring my younger sister and me. They aren't making dinner or packing our lunches for tomorrow. Our normally levelheaded, relaxed parents, who could rarely be bothered to worry over the scrapes and colds I'm often anxious about, look more afraid than Hannah and I have ever seen them. I stop folding the sleeping bag.

"Do you remember visiting the Twin Towers?" my mother asks. I'd been to New York with a friend in March.

"Yes," I answer, looking over her shoulder to the television, where the buildings are aflame and collapsing on a never-ending loop of newsreel. "They're gone," she tells us, disbelieving. My sister curls into my father's lap. I unzip the sleeping bag and huddle inside.

"And our country's going to go to war for it, just wait," my dad predicts knowingly. "People in Washington are going to use it as an excuse to bomb the hell out of those poor people."

"What people?" I ask, zipping the sleeping bag around my shoulders. I know I should be scared. I'm not. I'm just cold, all of a sudden. Annoyed no one has asked me about seventh grade today. And hungry for dinner.

"They have to find someone to blame," my mother answers, still not looking away from our small black television. The upstairs den is cold and my parents don't notice. I sink deeper into the hills of down-stuffed nylon.

"What can we do?" I ask quietly. My little sister looks strangely excited.

"Protest. Hope," my parents answer, a command that's also my name. Hope. "Pray that our country doesn't . . ." my dad drifts off. I get up, drag my sleeping back down the stairs to my basement bedroom, shuffle it under my bed, and get inside. Down in the damp darkness of my room, inside the hot, dry pocket of my sleeping bag, the new world can't touch me yet.

Trusting Eyes

Jami Kempen

After being addicted to prescription drugs for a few years, I looked into my daughter's face one day and saw her future if I continued. Abuse, drug seeking, mood swings, depression . . . surely she'd grow up thinking this was normal and an okay way to live. Her father and I are both addicts; it runs in families. Looking into her big, blue, trusting eyes, I realized that it was up to me to show her how to live; how to fight to overcome obstacles and not to lie down and die just because life is hard. Maybe, just maybe, if I saved myself from this addiction, I could spare her from going through it herself one day.

On August 3, 2009, my life changed drastically. I somehow found the courage to leave my drug-addicted husband and get myself clean. It was one of the hardest things I've ever had to go through. Now every day is a battle to make up for wasted years and get my life on a reasonable adult track, but I've remained clean and am honest about my progress and setbacks. Within this past year I have completed my GED and enrolled in college. I start in the spring.

I looked into my daughter's eyes and wanted to be better. For her.

Ingress/Egress

Jessica Anya Blau

Ingress

Okay, I'll do it," I said to my high school boyfriend, Mark, in the car on the way to the campsite. At that moment everything shifted. I was going from being a girl who wouldn't have sex to a girl who would.

We were camping on the cliffs of El Capitan beach in Santa Barbara. Jimmy had brought his parents' trailer, which was attached to a pickup truck. There were three couples: all of the boys juniors or seniors, all of the girls freshmen or sophomores. Everyone had done "it" except me. Hannah had even had an abortion already from her pregnancy with Kirk. Two years later, when he fell off the back of a truck and died, Hannah regretted that abortion. If only they'd kept it alive, she'd said, a part of Kirk would be here now.

We drank a case of Heineken by the campfire. By the time I'd finished my third beer (this was only the second time I'd ever had beer, and the most I'd ever had), I was ready to make good on my promise. Hannah and Kirk took their sleeping bags and hiked down to the beach. Jimmy and Janie set out their sleeping bags by the campfire. Mark and I went into the trailer. There was very little preliminary action. His clothes were off before we climbed into the loft bed. I helped him with my bra and wiggled out of my cotton underwear that caught on my big toe and stayed there.

"Okay," he said, "I'm totally going to do it now. I love you." And he stabbed his dull penis into my winking shut hole. There was no way it was going to slip in but he worked at it, bouncing on top of me, up and down, then back and forth, with unrelenting determination.

I was astounded that *this* was the thing people say feels so good. I mean, the entire world seemed delirious over this one act—at school boys boasted about having done it numerous times; parents flirted at parties, insinuating that this was what they were after; even some of the teachers at school seemed intent on letting students know that they wanted some of this. And, of course, so many girls' reputations dangled from the idea that they had happily done it. Yet it seemed so unpleasant, so lame, *so nauseating*.

"I'm going to be sick," I told Mark, and I slipped out from underneath him, ran out of the trailer, and leaned into the bushes, my bare butt waving in the air, where I vomited several times. If Jimmy and Janie heard or saw me, they didn't make a show of it. I slipped back into the trailer, without even a glass of water to clear the chunks of vomit clinging in my throat, and lay down for Mark, who picked up where he had left off.

"It'll get better next time," he said, after depositing a small puddle into my belly button. "You'll see."

The following Monday at school I saw myself as a different person walking down the halls. I passed Debbie, who had a reputation for loving sex so much that when she didn't have a boyfriend around, she'd stick pencils in her vagina. (I always wondered, *why pencils*, wasn't there something less pointy?) And there was Kristie who cried one day in the locker room when she told me that she had slept with not one of the L. brothers, but *all four.* Was I one of these girls now? There were five witnesses to my act (the mid-sex vomit had been discussed at breakfast), a number that in circles of gossip was equal to a billboard. Mark never *really* got it all the way in. I had found it terribly unpleasant. But that didn't matter. This was high school. Perception trumped reality. And I was no longer the same.

Egress

Something many parents don't tell you is that not everyone loves their baby at first sight. My first one came out looking like a pink, piggy little thing with a triangular dent in her forehead, a turned-up nose, and mucous smears on her cheeks. She rooted and squirmed and my then-husband exclaimed, "She's beautiful! She looks just like me!" I fully disagreed but said nothing as I stared at this creature who in my opinion did not resemble my husband at all but instead resembled my husband's father—a lovely, kind man who looked more than his age, with broken capillaries mapping his face, pale blue eyes, and shiny strings of hair across his head. Indeed, I was a bit freaked out to have just given birth to a porcine, seemingly boneless miniature of my sixty-year-old German Catholic father-in-law.

I was nursing, but let the nurses take the baby away between feedings so I could sleep, bleed and lactate, which is all one does following a delivery. Each time they returned the baby to me, I didn't quite recognize her. "Are you sure that's *my* baby," I'd ask? And the nurse would show me the ceramic lettered bracelet on her ankle that matched the one attached to my wrist. I come from a family of brown-eyed, brown to black-haired people. My ex-husband has brown hair and eyes. This pale, little creature just didn't look like she'd be mine.

And so I nursed her, and held her, changed her diapers and stared at her. Her neck was so tiny, her head so floppy, I thought of unfledged birds tossed out of the nest, marsupials that aren't ready to leave the pouch.

And then, the second full day in the hospital, she wouldn't stop suckling and she was cranky and kicking, her pink face fully flushing into a dappled red. Around nine o'clock that night, the doctor took her away to examine her. He came back without the baby.

"She's sick," he told me, "she has a fever and seems to have an infection. We need to put her in Intensive Care."

I can't tell you what my face looked like at the moment, but I can tell you that I was reading my reflection in the doctor's eyes. He was worried about me, about to call in the people with sedatives and white coats. It was clear I was absolutely stricken with fear and grief. My baby, who I at once recognized as someone who belonged to me but wasn't *mine* in the same way that my hand or foot was mine, had been taken away. And with the suddenness of a trap door dropping open, I was instantly, irrevocably, overwhelmingly in love with my daughter. My beautiful, exquisite little girl.

We both survived the week in ICU. Now, I can see that my love for her—and for her sister born five years later—is far too big for any words I might write. It was like that from the moment it began, the very second I fell in love.

Punchlines and Knockouts

Patrick Sauer

It was 1999. Three years out of grad school, recently turned thirty, just lost a job as a freelance fact-checker at the shuttered magazine *Maximum Golf* (Golf! Beer! Boobs! Golf!). Pile of unsold screenplays, loving wife who paid the rent, few prospects of fulfilling dream of becoming paid humor writer. Through an extremely tangential connection met Stephen Colbert, tried to get a job on *Strangers With Candy*. Exchanged contact info, sat on it until I had a great idea for *The Daily Show.*

As the author of *The Complete Idiot's Guide to Starting a Reading Group*, pitched Colbert an idea to parody Oprah's Book Club with underground cult favorites like "The Turner Diaries."

Colbert likes idea, puts me in touch with head writer/executive producer who asks me to send in three "Headline" bits. Gives me forty-eight hours. I hunker down for a weekend, write, rewrite, solicit feedback, polish, cross fingers and nervously hit send.

Two submission examples:

HEADLINE: JAMAICAN ME ANGRY
Subject: Violent riots between politically supported rival gangs in Bob Marley's hometown of Kingston.
Sample joke: "The peaceful smoke-filled bliss shattered this week when gunfire broke out between bitter rivals, the Buffalo Soldiers and the Dreadlock Rastas."

HEADLINE: SEND OUT THE CLOWNS
Subject: Retirement of beloved Chicago television clown Bozo.
Sample joke: "Professor Andy announced that he had accepted the position as chairman of the buffoonery department at Illinois State University."

Recreated half-remembered phone conversation with producer after the longest month-long waiting period of my life:

Producer: I like the "No Tear Gas, No Cry" line. . . . Payoff is weak. . . . Love the buffoonery bit. . . . Everyone would make the John Wayne Gacy joke. . . .

(I become aware I've stopped breathing.)

Producer: There's some good stuff in here, but to be honest, you have a similar comic voice as everyone in the room. I'm looking for someone with a completely different sensibility.

(It crosses my mind to say that I assumed sounding like *The Daily Show* was a requirement for getting hired, and that I was keeping my true out-of-left-field comedic voice quiet. That would have been 100 percent American hogwash. Thought flutters away. I U-turn and make a simple plea for employment.)

Me: Maybe I could be a writer's assistant of some kind, or help come up with scripts for the location shoots?
Producer: The producer and the correspondent mostly write the off-site stuff. We don't really have writer's assistants here. Sorry.
(Long pause.)
Me: Umm, well, thanks for taking the time to review my submission. Hopefully, our paths will cross again.
Producer: No problem. Keep at it.
(We hang up.)
Denouement: I sat there in silence for a few beats, expecting a common result, to be waylaid by the sting of rejection. It didn't take.
Moral of the Story: It wasn't that *the* moment had passed me by, but rather that it was *my* moment.

And it was all going to work out.

Obviously not today, but perhaps tomorrow. Or the day after that. Whenever. It was going to happen. I had stood in the ring with *The Daily Show*, emerged bloody and battered, but all I had to do was persevere and I'd be a winner. . . . To put it in easily understandable pop culture terms, I was following the *Rocky*-to-*Rocky II* arc. (Making Jon Stewart . . . my Adrian?) I saw my future. There would be no more big-picture self-doubt about career choice, no more scribe's day-to-day angst, no more pro bono pieces for "exposure." No more having my wife give me money before meeting friends in bars so it looks as if I am paying for drinks. No more questioning the value of a pricey post-grad degree. No more having to say "I'm hoping and try-ing to become a writer."

Ironically, after *The Daily Show* said no, I felt as if I could conquer the world. Every writer takes a beating, but this was a mere glancing blow on the road to superstar-Stephen-Colbert-dom. Made sense, since he was the one who got my foot in the door in the first place.

I may not have made it there—nor really anywhere for that matter—but in that moment of rejection, I knew I belonged.

Ten years later, I still watch *The Daily Show*. And wait.

"There would be no more big-picture self-doubt about career choice, no more scribe's day-to-day angst, no more pro bono pieces for 'exposure.'"

Head Case

Noah Scalin

said "Yes."

The challenge was silly, random, some would even say weird. And it turned my life upside down in the best possible way.

On June 2, 2007, I was celebrating my birthday in a park. As I walked across a patch of grass, one of the random thoughts that flitted through my head was this: *I should make a skull each day for one year.* Usually, I'm content to ponder odd thoughts for a moment, maybe share them with a friend, and then let them be on their way; this time was different.

About a month earlier, an art project I had been working on for many years fell apart, leaving me in a creative void. Despite having a job as a graphic designer, work that keeps me creatively engaged, I like to have an additional artistic outlet, ideally one not dictated by outside interests or a paycheck. It was in that light, on my birthday, that the notion of skull-making came into my head. I've had a thing for skulls since I was

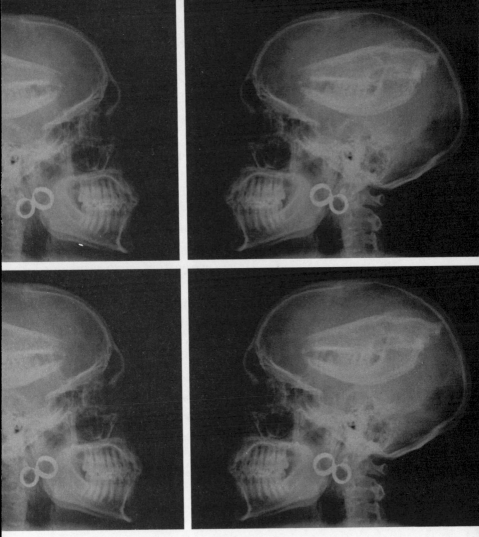

Skull #329: Some people definitely thought I should have my head examined during my year of skull-making. Consequently, I included an x-ray of my own head in the project, courtesy of a friend who teaches people how to use such equipment, and let me come in after hours. The skull in my head is from an opossum.

young, having grown up in an artistic household, where images of anatomy were not uncommon. And by the time this thought came to me I had several tattoos of them as well, so it was not an unusual image for me to have in my head. But instead of watching this specific thought about skulls float on, I invited it to stay for a while—365 days to be exact. I called it "Skull-A-Day."

Skull-A-Day officially began two days later when I cut a small skull out of orange paper, put it on my scanner, and uploaded the image to a blog (www.SkullADay.com). The entire process took around twenty minutes. By the end of the year, I was averaging four or five hours a day of work on the skulls, and sometimes as many as ten. Then something wild happened as other people heard about what I was up to: Skull-A-Day morphed from a personal outlet into a worldwide community project, one that ended up inspiring creativity in Marines in Iraq, encouraging inner-city teens in New York City to read, and helping primary school students in London learn about art. I've since made a book of the skulls, been invited to speak about the project across the world, and watched the project continue on as a place to share the hundreds of submissions of original art from people, young and old, who have been inspired to create and share their work every year since I finished. I remain amazed that such a small initial commitment transformed into something that has reverberated through my life, and the lives of others, ever since.

I'll never look at a random thought in the same way again.

In Pursuit of Optimism

Tony Schwartz

Partnerships are always challenging and ours was no different. The two of us had built a business together. We coauthored a best-selling book based on our work, helping organizations take better care of their employees' needs. But we ourselves weren't doing a very good job taking care of each other's. The irony wasn't lost on me.

Still, our shared mission was so strong that I had always assumed we'd find a way to work things out.

And then one morning, after a series of tough discussions, it became clear that there was no way forward.

Throughout my life, I had been someone who saw the cup as half empty. Pessimism, in my mind, was simply realism. For years, when I woke up, I very quickly found myself worrying about some challenge and imagining what might go wrong. It left me feeling drained and downbeat, but I had never been able to shake it.

In my work with leaders, however, I'd become very interested in the power to influence our perceptions. Specifically, I was taken with the distinction between the facts in any given situation, and the stories we tell ourselves about those facts. I came to recognize that we have a choice about how we interpret what happens to us, and that my instinctive default to the worst-case scenario wasn't serving me well.

I began experimenting with a new ritual. First thing each morning I would write down whatever I was worried about and its imagined negative conclusion. Then I tried to imagine a better outcome. I told myself an alternative story that was more hopeful and empowering, but still took into account the incontrovertible facts.

I did this every morning, dutifully, for several months, and it nearly always made me feel better. I began to notice that the negative outcome I initially feared almost never came to pass. And the positive one often did.

Then one morning I woke up, and sure enough, a challenging issue came into my mind. But this time, before a negative scenario could form, a more positive one occurred to me, effortlessly. It was a profound moment. In the days ahead, it was as if my whole center of gravity had shifted. Where clouds had always formed, now there was sun.

On that fateful day when my partnership broke up and my world threatened to turn upside down, I realized there was a positive way of looking at what had just happened. Here, now, was a chance to go off on my own and pursue the vision for our business that I'd been unsuccessfully trying to sell my erstwhile partner. This was the time for me to do something that was truly my own.

Today, I'm known for being a relentless optimist. Having transformed one of my darkest moments into a healthy business focused on doing something I love, I'm more convinced than ever that nothing is easy, but anything is possible.

Far Side

Katie Killacky

I remember the moment I started to believe in God. Not necessarily some bearded guy on a fluffy white cloud, but something beyond this earth; whatever it is waiting for us in the afterlife.

My grandmother was my best friend. I don't say that in a "we were very close" kind of way. I mean it as a young girl knows a best friend to be. From tea parties to singing around the house to making soup together, we were joined at the hip. Grandma had this way of making my four other siblings and me think we were each her favorite, but deep down, I knew I was her special one. Which is why in sixth grade when I heard the doctors telling my parents "Three, maybe four, months," I felt as though my world was coming to an end.

She lived out her days in our house with hospice workers, our angels, coming to take care of her. I would sit at her bedside after school and we would watch shows and talk about life and laugh—we laughed a lot. I grew up having this horrible fear of death and the unknown and Grandma knew that. I used to crawl into her bed in the middle of the night when I was scared about death. It didn't help the night I heard sounds coming from her room and snuck upstairs only to hear her now raspy voice pleading to God to just take her away from the pain.

More nurses and more morphine came and Grandma started to lose her memory about many things. In order to help Grandma keep track of the days, my mom got her one of those tear-off calendars. This particular one was *The Far Side,* so there was a joke for every day, and in the morning we would tear it off so Grandma had some sense of time and place.

One night I asked my mom if Grandma was scared.

"I think her biggest fear is that Maggie won't remember her." Maggie, my little sister, was only four at the time and also my grandmother's namesake. We all called her Maggie but Grandma called her Margaret, just like her. They had just begun having their tea parties together, but it suddenly occurred to me that Maggie would not remember Grandma as I knew her and I vowed to not let that happen.

Winter turned to spring and I came home from school to my grandfather in the kitchen. "I think Grandma's gone," he said and walked upstairs. Then the rest of the family came. Then hospice. Then the casseroles. And Grandma was gone.

The next few days were somber as we began cleaning out her room. Mom and Grandpa were quietly working away when I heard my mom say, "Oh . . . my . . . God. Would you look at this?"

My room was next door and I took a break from snuggling up on my bed crying to go see what she was talking about. In her hand was the next calendar joke we would have torn off. It was dated April 5, the day she died. There was a drawing of an old lady and a bird next to her in the window. The caption underneath read:

"I'm sorry, Margaret, but it's time I spread my wings and said good-bye."

Say what you will, but don't tell me everything is a coincidence. My grandmother either decided to play one last sick joke on us with her dark Irish humor or there was indeed something grander beyond this world. I still don't know what. But I know that that piece of paper was not just by chance, nor was it even a joke really. I view it as a way for her and Maggie to have a memory; a way for my family to have some peace of mind. And every time I start to lose my faith or get scared and want to crawl into her bed, it's a way to restore my faith that she always has been, and always will be, looking down on me.

Family Jewels

Gillian Laub

My grandfather wasn't well in the last year of his life, but he still had such a great sense of humor. At the time I took this photo of my grandparents I was single, and I remember thinking, *God, I hope one day I find a love like theirs.* They were married for more than sixty years and had so much warmth, joy, and humor. I can still hear my grandfather, leaning over and squeezing my grandmother, saying with such pride, "The family jewels!"

This moment reminds me of the most well-lived life: a man and woman in love, who put their family first. My grandfather had always said life was about "working hard and playing hard." That was his motto. He was my inspiration.

Grandma's Dildo

Sara Barron

There is much conversation and terror surrounding the idea that as women age they turn into their mothers. Just recently, a friend talked of stealing toilet paper from a public restroom. She'd instinctively thieved in this manner, thinking she'd use the score later as Kleenex.

"I just never thought it would happen to me," she cried.

I, sensitive as always, mentioned that I'd been left unmarred by such predictable behavior. "I'm a Blazer of Trails," I explained. "I've gone the more creative, more ambitious route of turning into my grandmother."

Twenty-two years ago, my grandfather Eugene passed away and widowed my grandmother Natalie. A year following his death, there was talk that perhaps Natalie might date again. A personal ad could be constructed. It could read something like, "Sixty-eight. Jewish. Single. Enjoys chocolate, Ensure and tit-twistingly awkward talks on the subject of progressive sexual politics."

The idea lost traction, however, as time revealed that my grandmother preferred self-inflicted solitude. As such, she became less adept at human interaction, and I tried and failed to mitigate all ensuing problems. I tried killing her with kindness, as it were. I baked her coffeecakes and chocolate-covered pretzels. I experimented with grandparental nicknames like "Grammy" and "Nana." I thought these might soften her up, and I was wrong. Her inter-generational nickname for me remained "a disappointment."

"You're a disappointment," she'd tell me. "Dating Pakistanis. Underemployed. Take a seat next to 'Grammy,' why don't you, and tell her where your standards are."

She spoke to inanimate objects.

She lived on Ensure and canned sardines.

She stocked a tube-sock in her bedside table, and a dildo in her tube-sock.

That last, most precious bit of information was reported by my brother Sam when, in the spring of my twenty-ninth year, he shared it an e-mail.

"I visited grandma today," it began, "and when I got there, she was like, 'Can you go upstairs and get my shoehorn? It's in the bedside table.' And I was like, 'Okay.' AND THEN IN THE BEDSIDE TABLE NEXT TO THE SHOEHORN WAS HER DILDO!!!! IN A TUBE-SOCK!!!! It was so fucking disturbing."

I found it fucking disturbing as well, though for different reasons than my brother. It wasn't so much that my grandmother had a dildo that disturbed me. It was the revelation of how like her I'd become. I too was single. I too lived alone. I too conversed with houseplants and sundry food items, including—among others—my beloved canned sardines. I was aware that these circumstances were making me less adept with other humans (a low point found me screaming at a Quiznos employee for having overcharged me for a hot sub) but still I convinced myself otherwise: that my attitude, generally, and my single gal's bitterness, specifically, were under control, and I'd attributed this, at least in part, to a dildo. A dildo kept beside my bed.

Of course, then my grandma's dildo did what grandmas' dildos do, and that's snap one to attention. Up until then, the transformation had been gradual enough to go unnoticed. But no more. I was twenty-nine, living alone, talking to houseplants and screaming at Quiznos employees. The fact that my hot pocket was popping was no proof that I was living like someone other than an eighty-nine-year-old. Something had to change. If not, the habits my grandmother indulged in her widowhood would be those I indulged for the length of a lifetime, and by age forty-one *I'd* be drinking Ensure. And amusingly, but still distinctly, racist.

So I did a thing my grandmother would never do. I went onto OKCupid, to create an online dating profile. "Twenty-nine. Jewish. Single," I wrote. "Enjoys cooking—for you, whoever you are!—and tit-twistingly awkward talks on the subject of my G-ma's masturbation."

Having gone bold with "G-ma's masturbation," I closed with a vanilla coating: "I love music, reading, and adventure!" I basked in the glow of having been proactive and, in celebration, flash-fried up some fresh sardines. Later did I dream of just rewards: A Jew (reformed) possessing a low-brow sensibility who, despite the obvious unlikelihood, looked strikingly like Djimon Honsou. Failing that, anyone would do; *anyone*. But her dildo-assisted solitude would, finally, not be mine.

Oprah Calling

Ray Richmond

In early October 2004 my thoughts were consumed by the race for president of the United States between President G. W. Bush—gunning for his second term—and Sen. John Kerry. The contentious campaigns had by then reached the "Your Mama, and your Daddy too!" stage when name-calling supersedes anything resembling constructive-issues dialogue. Only a superhero could save this thing from sinking further into the muck.

Where have you gone, Oprah Winfrey? Our nation turns its jaundiced eyes to you.

This was the question I'd raised that very day in my weekly *Hollywood Reporter* column, "The Pulse." Moreover, I posed plenty of others: Why wouldn't Oprah discuss the presidential race on her show? Why didn't she have the candidates on to answer questions weightier than, "Why don't you smile more, senator?" She seemed to be willfully disengaged from the forthcoming election. Didn't she care about America?

Around 2:30 that afternoon my home office phone rang.

"Ray Richmond, please."

"Speaking."

"It's Oprah Winfrey."

It was instantly clear this was no imposter. That distinctive voice. Her Highness, inexplicably and surrealistically on Line 1. No assistant announcing, "Please hold for Oprah." Just her.

"Hello Ray," she said coolly.

God called me Ray! God called me Ray!

"Um . . . hello, Oprah."

"I'm here with four of my producers joining us on this call. We read your column today with great interest. And we were wondering what you might suggest we do on the show to involve the presidential candidates."

"Seriously?"

I didn't realize I'd spoken aloud until she replied, "Oh absolutely."

My face grew suddenly flushed. It felt like an out-of-body experience, as if I were hovering over my shell-shocked self. I put down the phone for a second to shake loose the mental cobwebs and take stock. Yes, I was conscious. Yes, I was about to enter an *Oprah* story meeting as an unpaid consultant.

I had abruptly transformed from a slovenly freelance journalist in his underwear into the Go-to Guy for Queen Oprah I.

But wait.

"So then let me get this straight. Do you really care what I have to say or is this you just yanking my chain with, like, 'OK Mister Smarty Pants, what bright ideas have you got, hmmm?'"

I frankly couldn't believe my audacity, that I had the presence of mind to speculate aloud if this were just a sporty opportunity to belittle and intimidate some media dweeb.

"No, we really care what you have to say," Oprah assured me. "Your column got us to thinking. So what are your thoughts?"

It was utterly inconceivable. She had deemed my judgment officially worthy of . . . well . . . something. Life had handed me Oprah, so I made Oprah-ade, proceeding over the next fifteen minutes to tell her and her production minions how to run their show. A week with Bush. A week with Kerry. Lots of audience questions. Nationally televised town-hall meetings.

They all seemed to embrace what I had to say. Oprah thanked me for my time and my ideas. She promised to give them serious consideration. She bid good-bye.

And then she proceeded to do nothing.

Shoot forward to May 2007. Oprah announced that she was endorsing Illinois senator Barack Obama for president in 2008. Not only did she leap into the election fray; she did it with eighteen months to spare. She became a one-woman promotional machine for the man who'd win the White House.

Why the sudden political passion and zealotry from a woman who previously kept partisanship and TV as separate as church and state? One could guess that it stemmed from Obama's race, or his Illinois roots, or his Kennedy-esque youth and vitality.

Or one might step back to a certain telephone conversation in October 2004 with a journalist who called Oprah out, stoked her conscience, unchained her accountability . . . and left her determined to do things differently the next time. Were you to reach the latter conclusion while at the same time crediting Oprah's vocal support with an essential assist in Obama's ascension to the Oval Office, it would mean that I personally altered the very direction of the Free World.

Yeah, let's go with that.

You're welcome.

Vietnam, Revisited

Karol Nielsen

I was six months old when my father left for Vietnam, as a first lieu-
tenant with the 101st Airborne, the Screaming Eagles. My brother
ran through the house like "Soupy-man," cape draped over his shoulders: "My daddy fly up in the air, my daddy fly up in the air!" I had
no idea who my father was when he came home a year later, inching
over the backseat of the car to sit between him and my chatty brother. I have no memory of this. I was too little then, but it is ingrained
in me like my other memories of my father and his tour in Vietnam.
These are collective memories, family memories, the quiet truths of
war borne by all of us, carried and curated as if our own. Then it was
Vietnam, now it is Afghanistan, but war is all the same. When I saw
a *New York Times* photo essay about one battalion's deployment to
Afghanistan, I wrote a poem in a series of tweets, moved by a sad man
holding his baby, hugging his wife. As I looked at this man cradling
his child, I thought of how my life changed as an infant, how those
first six months of innocence were cut short, how Vietnam made me
who I am.

My father used to look at the stars
and think of me, my brother,
my mother. In short shorts.

In Vietnam, my father "saw some shit."
In the central highlands, along the central coast,
by the Cambodian border. I was a baby then.

I have no memory of an innocent time,
before I carried his war stories
in my head, like a movie I'd seen.

War makes no sense, my father always said.
We watch the *NewsHour* together, to honor the dead.
It ends quietly. Like the silence of those who can no longer
speak.

Conversation with My Dad

Ashley Allen

packed my bags haphazardly, not really caring about the clothes I was bringing. Most of them I left for my sister, since soon none of them would fit me anyway. Dad was waiting downstairs alone. Alyson, my older sister, had left for school hours ago, and my stepmother was out of town. Her stipulation was that I be gone by the time she got back. They could've put me on a plane or train, but my dad chose instead to drive me the ten hours to Ohio. It was an odd choice for him to make, I thought. The car ride was bound to be painfully and awkwardly silent.

We rode in the car for three hours without saying a word. Long silences were not uncommon where my introverted father was concerned, and he was especially uncomfortable with conversations of any emotional kind. I opened my mouth a dozen times to say something but never spoke. If he wasn't asking questions, why should I give him answers? Regardless, even if he made the predictable queries, the answers weren't very enlightening. Yes, it was my first time. No, we didn't use anything. Yes, I knew better. No, I had no idea what I was going to do with the rest of my life.

"You'll come home to Ohio," my mother had said on the phone. "You'll have the baby here—I know of a high school program for expecting girls. And, of course, we'll help you raise it." These words were uttered between her sniffles and sobs, but the crying only lasted a few minutes. Maybe she was in shock. But it was more likely that, with four young kids of her own to take care of, she was comfortable with crisis. Plus, it meant she was getting me back.

When I returned to the car with a bottle of Sprite and a box of Ritz crackers, Dad wasn't in the driver's seat. I spotted him in a phone booth with his head bent close to the receiver. Breaking open a sleeve of crackers, I watched him shake his head rigorously as he talked to my stepmother. They were fighting. This was a rare occurrence, and I felt guilty.

Dad walked slowly to the car.

"Debbie?" I asked, needlessly. "Mm-hmm," he grumbled. I took a deep breath as we both strapped on our seatbelts. "Dad? I'm so sorry," I said. He didn't look up. "I didn't mean for this to happen." Minutes of silence passed, and the despair was overwhelming. I thought of the past few agonizing weeks. The day I skipped school and took the pregnancy test alone, my hand shaking as I held the results. The day I first felt the morning sickness, at seven weeks along, and vomited in the smoke-filled girls' bathroom. The day I'd walked down our neighborhood street, as if in a bubble, and watched kids playing, people mulching their flowerbeds. I'd sat down on the curb and squeezed my eyes shut, wishing myself out of my own body.

I searched for words to bridge the gap between Dad's disappointment and my desperation, but in the end, I didn't need to.

"I love you," Dad said, his voice cracking. "And we're going home." He pulled the car off the next exit and headed back the way we'd come. I started to shake and cry, and he reached an arm over to comfort me. Finally.

In the hours that led us back home, he told me about Debbie's miscarriages. If I lived with them, she would be tormented by my pregnancy. She already was. Against her wishes, he was taking me back so that I could weigh my choices. This was the first time he'd spoken to me like an adult, so I answered in kind. I talked about Mom's alcoholism, a secret I'd buried for so long, and described how hard it had been to leave her. I couldn't bear going back.

The decision was an excruciating one. After the abortion, my conversations with my father eventually trickled back to one-word grunts and perfunctory report card lectures. In twenty years, I've never had a conversation with him matter more.

Season's Greetings

Ellen Jantzen

Before Christmas 2010, whenever I visited my mother-in-law at the Breese Nursing Home in Illinois, I would avert my eyes when passing residents. Somehow it seemed that the aging process could be "caught" and if I didn't make eye contact I would be immune. As I enter mid-life, I see the end approaching much more quickly than I had when I was younger. I see the process, very graphically, at the nursing home; the physical abilities lost and the mental faculties fading; the wrinkles, the gray hair.

I was reluctant to attend the Christmas party and only did so as emotional support for my husband. Then something transformative happened as I observed the humanity still residing inside these aging bodies as they interacted with their families. So I took out my camera.

I took these photos without a flash in order to be as unobtrusive as possible, and shot them in such a way that faces would be disguised to help maintain privacy. What's not hidden in these photographs is joy, humor, and a lust for life.

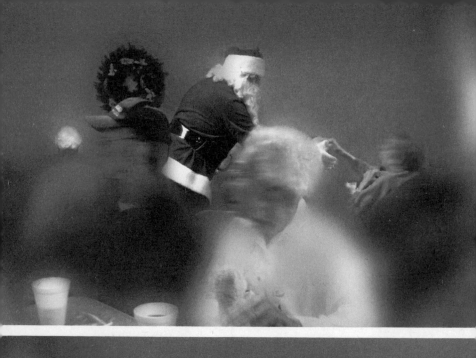

Revisionist History

Catherine Gilbert Murdock

I was maybe twenty-three years old. I'd taken a year off from grad school to edit a corporate history; "editing" in this case meaning "wheedling essays from two dozen obdurate contributors and then halving the word count after removing all references to interdepartmental squabbling." At least the warring factions agreed that I was far too artless to be sucked into their battles.

I did score a little coup, however, in engineering the hiring of a book designer I'd known for years, a woman I adored for her competence and wit. One day Adrianne and I were working together on page proofs. She pointed to two words disheveling her layout. "Can you get rid of those?" she asked. "Tweak it somehow?" So I deleted an adverb here, shortened a verb there. . . . I can't remember precisely how I compressed the paragraph, but I will never forget the sensation.

Before then, I had always viewed revision as akin to playing music. You start at the beginning and bang your way through to the end: a plodding, listless, linear process. At this moment, however, I realized that editing isn't linear at all. In fact, it's nothing less than a highly entertaining puzzle in which you get to maneuver all the bits:

This prose should go *here,* not there! Inject that adverb into the verb! The phrase doesn't fit: gone! If you're diligent and thoughtful and, yes, playful enough, you can always make it better.

Perhaps it was Adrianne's approval that made this so clear, or the fact that I love Sudoku but suck at piano; I don't know. The months I'd spent halving all those essays doubtless contributed. But to this day, whenever I have a particularly satisfying experience of polishing prose, I remember her sunny studio and how happy I felt at that instant, when one big piece of the puzzle fell into place at last.

Forgiven

Jennifer Thompson

In January 1985 I sat in the Alamance County Courthouse, in North Carolina, and listened to a jury announce that Ronald Cotton was guilty of first-degree rape, first-degree burglary and first-degree sexual assault. My heart gave a heavy sigh and for the first time in six months I felt a small window of safety. He was a monster that had come into my life uninvited and shattered everything I had worked for, planned on, and hoped for. I wanted him to die, in the most painful and horrible way. I would pray for this but, in the meantime, life in prison would have to be his punishment.

Over the next few months I somehow put the few pieces of my broken life together, but it was not without large amounts of self-destruction and fear. I would move on, but the horrors of that July night followed me wherever I went. I could not go far enough to escape the hell of what Ronald Cotton had done to me. That girl, Jennifer Thompson, had been left behind and in her place were but hollow fragments that at times were unrecognizable to me. It was only blind hate and rage that allowed me to know I was still alive.

Years passed. I began to work, fell in love, and, in 1988, got married. By the spring of 1990, my life took a beautiful turn and I gave birth to triplets. Morgan, Blake, and Brittany burst into the world with all the wonder and amazement new life takes on, times three. *God loves me,* I thought. He blessed me with these babies because he trusted me to take care of them. I was worthy and valuable again. My energies focused on my children yet somewhere deep inside it gave me pleasure to know that Ronald would not have this. He would never hold his baby, love a woman, or see the light of freedom again. As I would pray for the safety of my babies, I would still wish for Ronald to meet a cruel end to his pathetic life. People who did horrible things deserved terrible endings. It was only fair.

Eleven long years went by since the crime, and my life was busy with three five-year-old preschoolers. Laundry and skinned knees replaced old fear and insecurities. And then the phone rang in the spring of 1995 and I heard the reassuring voice of Mike Gauldin, the detective from my rape case, asking if he could come into town and visit me. His voice had been the one thing that had kept me together during those dark days. I looked forward to seeing him again.

But he came with the news that Ronald Cotton and his attorneys were seeking a test, a DNA test, to prove his innocence. The outrage shocked me. He was guilty. Everyone knew it. The judge, jury, community, and DA's office all knew it. *I knew it.* I did not want to revisit the pain. "Fine. Run the test, please," I said. "But I cannot do this again. I have a life now." I was not concerned about the results because I'd seen his face in my nightmares every night for the last four thousand days. Ronald Cotton was a rapist. That was certain.

Less than three months later, Mike and the assistant district attorney of Alamance County stood in my kitchen to deliver the news. The stress on their faces told me something would once again come and shatter my life.

Ronald Cotton was innocent. His DNA did not match the biological evidence from the rape kits. Instead, the DNA matched a serial rapist, Bobby Poole, who had been in the same prison as Ronald, and Ronald had tried to tell anyone who would listen that we had gotten it all wrong. I was paralyzed with guilt, shame, and abject fear. All these years I had been wrong. I had wished for his death. I wanted him to feel pain. What was I to do? How much anger must he feel? When and how will he act out his revenge? Was my family safe?

It took me two years before I could ask Ronald for something that he had waited more than a decade to receive. As I sat in a church not far from where I had been raped thirteen years before, Ronald walked into the room. Through tears, I asked if he could ever forgive me.

Ron did the one thing I had not expected. "I forgive you," he said. " I am not angry at you. You made a mistake because you are human. Do not be afraid of me, I will never hurt you. I want you to be happy, and I want to be happy. Live a good life, Jennifer!"

The man I had prayed would die would now teach me how to live. Ronald taught me more that afternoon than I have ever learned in any church. He showed me grace, mercy, and forgiveness, and unlocked my spirit so I could live a life of joy, peace, and love.

Ronald and I have become best friends and advocates for judicial reform. He is now one of my richest blessings. I cannot imagine my life without him.

Second Chance

Jerry Ma

Moving On

Mary Valle

On December 31, 2010, I moved a box of my dead brother Michael's stuff into my basement. It had been sitting upstairs in my spare bedroom since he died in 2005. I was in Baltimore, Maryland—the ever-hopeful, ever-declining Rust Belt city where I've been hiding out for the past ten years. I live with my husband and daughter in a fixer-upper in a nice, leafy neighborhood. Moving here from Los Angeles was my idea, as it's about as far away from California as one can possibly get in every sense except the physical. It was a good choice: Baltimore's decay and relative obscurity have supported my vital brooding, moping, and whole-body scowling perfectly.

I acquired this box of Michael's belongings when he died, alone, in Florida, of AIDS. I loved him a great deal—at times, more than anything, even though I very frequently hated him, and, indeed, wished him dead. I stored these reminders of him in an extra bedroom that I then tried to avoid. Finally, years later, after cleaning out my basement, I entered the spare bedroom and, with no fanfare, transferred the box downstairs. Anyone who saw the event would have thought: *There's a woman moving a plastic storage bin into the basement, noth-*

ing to see here. But, in fact, this was momentous. In addition to regaining my extra room upstairs, I'd decided that a memoir I'd been pitching—about my intense relationship with my brother, including the period that I moved in to help take care of him, how he went totally insane and *then* my own total mental breakdown and near-death experience during two years of cancer treatment—was no longer the story I wanted to write. All the anger and bitterness and grief I'd been carrying around were gone; I let them fly away like a great bouquet of helium balloons.

What happens when you let go of the story you've always told yourself? I'm about to find out.

 What happens when you let go of the story you've always told yourself?"

Four Long Years

Dar Wolnik

Lost just about everything in four inches of water in August 2005. Came back to pull out a few things, said goodbye to that home, spent the next few years working hard to help rebuild my city. Lived in many different neighborhoods, taking friends' offers of empty apartments or places to put a FEMA trailer. Waited for my old apartment to be ready, only to realize ultimately that it never would be because the landlady would not fix it right and wanted twice the rent. Almost built my own house but decided not to. Found an apartment in my favorite area of the city that was quiet, had a small yard for my dog and a nice porch to sit and watch the birds. Painted it, bought stuff for it, puzzled over what should go where. Finally, on a warm, sunny day in October 2009, I had no more errands to do. Unlocked my bike and rode to nearby City Park. Crested the Dreyfous Bridge, watching the fishermen to the right; then descended, looking at the sculpture garden to the left. Picked up speed and suddenly felt as if I had just fully woken up after four long years. Could hear every happy sound, as if my ears had been unclogged. Everything looked brighter. It took a few minutes but I finally realized: the shock had just worn off.

Birth

John B. Carnett

As a photographer I'd always insulated myself against the world. The camera is the buffer, that something between myself and the moment in front of me. The wind, the cold, the gesture, the reality of the moment is frozen for that fraction of time that the camera converts 3-D space to 2-D. It happens so fast, and so often, it's a place in which I'm quite comfortable. But all those moments of buffered conversion are actually lost moments of real time: I am not present. Only later when the image is processed does the moment return. That place where I was, the very moment that I was absent, reappears. When my first son, Quint, was born I had my camera and made this picture. When my second son, Henry, was born I owned the moment itself.

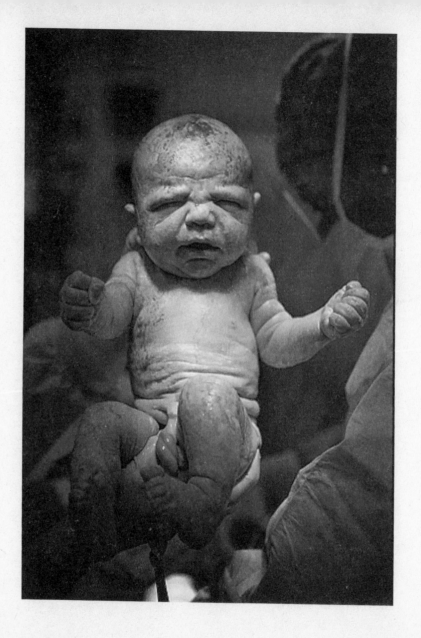

The Moth and the Window

Stephen Tobolowsky

I came out to Los Angeles to become an actor and it was all so impossible. I couldn't get a job. I couldn't get an agent. I couldn't even work for free. I performed in one show where I had to pay the producer a hundred dollars to cast me. It was not money well spent. Opening night no one was in the audience.

One bright spot was that I made friends with other struggling actors. One of them knew Pat Riley, the new coach for the Los Angeles Lakers. That season the Lakers made it into the playoffs and my friend got me a ticket to sit in the tenth row to see the game with him. I was in heaven.

My car was a dented Oldsmobile that was on its last legs. It had no heater, nor working windshield wipers. The windows were of the hand-crank variety and the front driver's window was permanently stuck in the down position. Well, not completely down. About one inch of window peeked from the bottom, but it was hardly any protection from the elements. Whenever I drove anywhere the only thing I had to keep me warm was moving to the rock and roll on the radio.

It was freezing that night on the way to the arena. I switched the radio from "Shake It Up" by the Cars to the game. It was about fifteen minutes before tip-off. I pulled behind a long line of cars headed into a parking area. That's when I noticed I was not alone. There was a big moth in the car fluttering around my face. I swatted at it and tried to encourage it to fly out of the permanently open window. Remarkably, it flew into the only sliver of window that was closed and flew back in my face.

I spoke to the moth with quiet authority. "Go on. Get out of here. Get." It was now ten minutes before the tip-off and the line of cars hadn't budged. I stuck my head out the window and yelled, "Let's go!" I honked once and sat back in the car. The moth fluttered around my head and again I tried to knock it out the window. Again, he kept banging into the one inch of glass, missing the opening again and again. I muttered, "Stupid, idiotic moth. What a moron."

On the radio they started introducing the players. Now I was in a panic. There had to be some sort of problem up ahead. Maybe someone didn't have change. Maybe the parking lot was full. I started honking my horn and yelled, "Come on! Move it!" The moth tried to fly up my nose again. I said, "Look Moth, you have the *entire window*!

"*The moth tried to fly up my nose again. I said, 'Look Moth, you have the entire window! It is completely open! Go! Or I will kill you.' (I often talk tough to insects.)*"

It is completely open! Go! Or I will kill you." (I often talk tough to insects.)

The game started. I screamed. I finally got out of my car to see what the hold up was and then I saw—to my horror—I had been waiting in a line of *parked cars*. I had been honking and yelling at no one. Upon further examination there wasn't even a gate up ahead. The entrance to the arena was only a product of my wishful thinking.

The moth flew into the window once again. Then I saw it. In that one moment, we were exactly the same, the moth and I. He couldn't see the open window. I couldn't see that I was behind a line of parked cars. It was all a matter of point of view.

Since then, there have been many walls thrown at me by life. Hardships. Setbacks. But because of my friend, the moth, I learned that a wall may not be a wall; from a different angle, it could be a bridge.

Tomorrowland

Rebecca Woolf

Daisy, F3," my son Archer says as we pull into our parking spot. Disneyland's about to open and we've arrived, just the two of us, our last hoorah before school starts.

The alarm goes off and I pull the pillow tightly over my head. My husband, Hal, offers to wake the kids so I roll over, fall back asleep until Archer's voice wakes me, this time for good. "Hi, Mommy. It's kindergarten day."

Before we go on any rides, Archer tells me he wants to watch "the rapids coaster."

"It will only take a minute," he says, but an hour passes and we're still watching. He points and studies and tilts his head, trying to understand why one raft is *here* when another is *there*, tracing time with his finger as he calculates distance and studies the faces of the hundreds of people screaming down the falls. Every few minutes I ask Archer if he's ready to get on the ride.

"Not yet," he tells me but I'm getting impatient. Bored. I cross my legs and watch him, pick my fingernails and wait.

And then . . .

"Hey, Mom. Want to go on this ride with me?"

. . . yes.

He climbs into the raft first and I follow. We are surrounded by a group of seriously prepared strangers covered in plastic to keep their clothes dry. Archer flashes me a look and I tell him that, no, I don't have plastic in my purse.

He tells me that it's okay, the sun will dry us, and for a second, I feel as if I'm the child.

When the ride ends our hair is drenched, shoes full of water, clothes soaked through. We walk like ducks to the bathroom where we dry our shoes under the electric hand driers before unfolding our soggy map and pointing out a new destination.

I adjust his collar, button the three buttons on his shirt, help him with his sweater, tie his shoes. Archer shakes his head back and forth making it very difficult for me to get that last button. I'd tell him to stop but he's so excited, so I say nothing, move with his jumps and jolts and sways, try to fit the button through the buttonhole until finally . . .

"Got it."

It's 7:12 and I want to be out the door in eighteen minutes. Hal and I are still in our pajamas but at least Archer is dressed.

"You look very handsome," I say.

Archer makes a face. "No I don't."

He does.

We're on the retro car ride, Autopia, for the third time. Archer's driving but he doesn't know my foot is on the gas. He's too busy trying to make the car move on his own. He's mastered the art of steering without bumping against the track. It only took him two times to figure it out. Two times and forty minutes of watching from the sidelines.

"I can steer really well, Mama," he says.

"Indeed you can."

We're in the car now. We've managed to get dressed with one minute to spare. Archer requests his favorite song and I turn the volume up as Hal backs out the driveway.

At the stoplight I turn down the music, tell Archer about my first day of kindergarten. I was wearing a white dress with blue stripes and my teacher's name was Ms. Parish. Hal tells him about his first day of kindergarten and Archer nods, sort of listening, mostly studying the new route from our house to school.

"Light's green, Dad. You can go now."

I take him on Small World because it's my favorite. He tells me he'd rather ride the submarines, but I say I can't because I'm afraid of confined spaces and would get sick if I went inside.

"Then let's go on Small World," he agrees.

We share a cotton candy and laugh at the wooden frogs.

On the playground, the parents gather with tired eyes, watching nervously, sad and scared and excited and overwhelmed. Some of the children cling to their parents, or at least stay close. Not Archer. He could have easily said good-bye at the car and walked himself to class. I'm glad he's excited but there's a part of me that hoped he would cling to me, at the very least, hold my hand. Instead, I hold his backpack.

I feel bad because I left his sweatshirt in the car. I hadn't realized we'd still be here. Thought we'd stay for the day and be home for dinner. It's dark now and getting cold so I give Archer my cardigan. He puts it on and laughs as it falls down to the tops of his shoes.

"It's a little big," he says.

Archer drags me toward Tomorrowland, where a man at a booth is selling light sticks and things that flash like strobes. I offer to buy him one if I have enough money—I only have ten dollars left in my wallet. Archer gets so excited he starts jumping up and down but can't decide which light he wants until . . .

"THAT ONE!" he screams.

"How much for the light saber?" I ask the man at the booth.

"Ten dollars," he says.

Archer looks at me and smiles.

The fireworks are about to start so I carry him on my back and we run, dodging strollers and families clutching giant stuffed Mickeys. Archer wants me to put him down, says he can walk on his own, but I don't want him to miss this.

"We're almost there," I say.

And then they start. We watch together as the fireworks explode and he's smiling at them with his hands against my neck, light saber to the sky. He puts his head on my shoulder and the lights dance across his face. The music swells, all songs from my childhood Yesterdayland. Archer's never heard them before but he likes that the fireworks make a heart in the sky. I haven't seen the fireworks at Disneyland since I was a little girl and have no recollection of them being this magical. I urge them to go on forever.

And then . . .

"Let's go home."

"Really? You don't want to stay a little longer?"

"No, Mom. I'm ready to go."

Archer points his light saber toward the entrance as we make our way back through the crowd.

We try to walk him into class but he takes his backpack from my hands and scurries ahead to join his classmates on the rug. I wave to the back of his head.

"Good-bye," I say.

On the way back to the car Archer insists on walking, using his light beam as a sort of cane he hits against the pavement. "Crack, crack, craaaaaack," it goes, smacking and dragging until at last we arrive at the car.

And then, as if by magic, the light beam stops blinking. Perhaps he broke it hitting it so many times or the battery died or it was just its time. Clutching the broken beam, Archer bursts into tears. I wait for him to fall asleep before I do the same. I'm crying and I can't stop. Because the day is over. Because the light went out. Because our moment has passed.

Because all moments do.

Me and my brother having another of our fights.
It had been coming. He punches me,
I almost pull out a knife.

—*Adriano Morae*

My husband and I had recently decided to get
divorced, and I was talking to my best friend
over margaritas about how long it had been
since I had been kissed.

—*Molly Meyer*

*The Dungeons and Dragons dungeon blueprints and
twelve-sided dice consumed us during recess.*

—*Andrew Shaffer*

As I departed Paris, my boyfriend took
this photo of me from a train on the
tracks at Gare de l'Est.

—*Lara Swimmer*

Photograph courtesy of Lara Swimmer

My husband's mother had a philosophy
on illness: Take two aspirins and you'll
be fine in the morning.

—*Mary Ellen Marks*

On the balmy Honolulu evening after I was born,
it was Poker Night at my Uncle Danny's house, and
my old man was passing out cigars to the guys.

—*Jace Albo*

Something magical happened: Robert Braudt landed on my Facebook wall.

—*Nicola Behrman*

The text my aunt sent me at midnight read, "I think Nana will go soon."

—*Adam Roth*

*You are extraordinarily beautiful. I noticed that
right away. That's why I took your picture.*

—*Judy Clement*

When Marcel learns that his beloved grandmother has no
chance of recovery in Proust's *In Search of Lost Time*, the
discovery pierces the carefully ordered world of routine he has
constructed to get him through each day.

—*Ben Wieder*

*Still flat as a board, but tall and willowy, at fifteen
my hipless torso and ribbon legs only predicted the
shape I would eventually own in adulthood.*

—*Cathy Alter*

The oblong green-and-white pill slid down my throat.
—*Kelley Jhung*

I had spent the morning and the previous day with a young man
who was scheduled for execution by the state of Texas.
—*Pamela Skjolsvik*

I lost my middle daughter, Gabrielle, when she passed
away from leukemia at the age of twenty-seven.
—*Denise Rich*

There are only two ways to live: for
literature, or as literature.
—*Joshua Coen*

I never knew how badly I wanted to get married until I
changed my Facebook status to "engaged."
—*Melinda Hill*

*Three days past my due date, with our mothers and their
nervous energy overcrowding our 1,200-square-foot condo and
tons of labor-inducing wives' tales tried and failed, we placed
a desperate call to our midwife.*
—*Shauna Green*

Until I was ten, I did not understand
people died of natural causes.
—*Porochista Khakpour*

I couldn't get it up.
—*James Franco*

Everyone Has a Moment. What's Yours?

Share your story—in words or images—
on *SM!TH Magazine*'s The Moment project.
www.smithmag.net/themoment

Join our Facebook page for updates on the Moment Project.
facebook.com/themomentproject

Tweet your moment with the hashtag #mymoment.

Acknowledgments

All books are collaborations. Books that have more than a hundred authors are something more.

The Moment was born at *SMITH Magazine* storytelling events around the country, where people came up to me again and again and said, "I have the most amazing story to tell you about this one thing that changed my life." When the notion of life-changing moments became a new story project on SMITHmag.net, the members of the *SMITH* community did what they always do: They shared incredible stories—honestly, passionately, authentically. The *SMITH* community not only makes the site hum each day, they have made manifest the site's tagline from the day we launched on January 6, 2006: Everyone has a story. In these past six years, the *SMITH* community has continued to expand, from the many people I've met in person at story events across the country to the legions of people running bookstores, libraries, poetry slams in bars, and anywhere else a good story is likely to break out.

To the authors featured in this book, I am so grateful. Sharing the kind of personal story usually reserved for the closest of friends and family can be a frightening thing. We had more exceptional submissions than we could fit into this book, and choosing which ones to include was not easy. As such, we've created a special section on *SMITH* (smithmag.net/themoment) featuring many stories that space constraints forced us to leave out of the print edition.

The book itself came together after many conversations with Kate Hamill, the inventive editor who brought *SMITH Magazine*'s first online project, *Six-Word Memoirs*, to print. Editors Julia Cheiffetz and Katie Salisbury helped shape the work further, and Harper's Michael Signorelli finessed it to the finish line. Thanks as well to everyone at HarperCollins, and to ICM's Kate Lee, who is a trifecta of agent, wordsmith, and friend.

I gave *SMITH* contributing editor Vivian Chum the vaguest of challenges—seek out interesting people and ask them to share a "moment." Vivian's deft eye and ability to charm the busiest of brains to contribute a story was invaluable. Associate editor Meredith Sires thrust herself into every aspect of *The Moment* and was invaluable throughout the process, as was my copy guru, Jonathan Lesser, as well as Meghan Milam and Liz Crowder. Any editor of an anthology of five pieces—or, in this case, 125—would be fortunate to have Patrick Price as an editor on his team: He's a master at his craft. Among many others, I'm so appreciative of Tim Barkow, Rachel Fershleiser, Jeff Newelt, John House, David Boyer, Jeff Cranmer, Cheryl Della Pieta, Gary Belsky, Mary Elizabeth Williams, Rosally Sapla, Abby Ellin, Jim Gladstone, Don Hazen, Michael Callahan, Danielle Claro, Lisa Qiu, and Rob McKay, all of whom have provided support throughout this and many other *SMITH* projects.

Words of gratitude are not enough to offer to my wife, Piper Kerman, who had a front-row seat to the book-making circus, and whose support has kept me sane through its many acts. Finally, thanks to our new son, Lukas, whose moments arrive each and every day.

Larry Smith

Contributors

Caroline Paul ("Flash," pg. 1) is a journalist and author of *Fighting Fire*, a memoir of her time as a San Francisco firefighter, and *East Wind, Rain*, about the villagers of an isolated Hawaiian island whose lives are forever changed when a plane crash-lands nearby.

A. J. Jacobs ("Chalk Face," pg. 4) is the best-selling author of *The Year of Living Biblically* and *My Life as an Experiment*.

Dean Karnazes ("Shot," pg. 6) is a bestselling author and was named by *Time* magazine as one of the "Top 100 Most Influential People in the World." In 2006, he accomplished what many thought was impossible by running fifty marathons in fifty states in fifty consecutive days.

Mo Clancy ("The Envelope," pg. 8) was once a trend forecaster for Fortune 500 fashion and consumer brands. He now focuses on modern artifacts and Mayan culture.

Diane Ackerman ("Love in a Time of Illness," pg. 12) is the author of *A Natural History of the Senses, One Hundred Names for Love, The Zookeeper's Wife*, and many other books of poetry and prose.

Paul West ("Subdued by Stroke," pg. 14) is a writer and poet. West's literary craft has earned him the American Academy of Arts and Letters Literature Award (1985), the Lannan Prize for Fiction (1993), the Grand Prix Halperine-Kaminsky Award (1993), and three Pushcart Prizes (1987, 1991, 2003).

Laurie David ("Table Time," pg. 16) is an environmental activist, a trustee on the Natural Resources Defense Council, and an Academy Award–winning producer of *An Inconvenient Truth*, the coauthor of *The Down-to-Earth Guide to Global Warming*, and most recently, the author of *The Family Dinner: Great Ways to Connect with Your Kids, One Meal at a Time*.

Summer Pierre ("Tattoo," pg. 18) is the author of *The Artist in the Office: How to Creatively Survive and Thrive Seven Days a Week*. She lives in Brooklyn, NY with her family.

Michael Paterniti ("The Killer in Me," pg. 19) is the cofounder of the nonprofit writing center, The Telling Room, in Portland, Maine, and author of *Driving Mr. Albert: A Trip Across America with Einstein's Brain*. His work has appeared in *Harper's*, the *New York Times Magazine*, *Esquire*, and *GQ*.

Amy Sohn ("To Worry," pg. 22) is author of the novels *Prospect Park West*, *My Old Man*, and *Run Catch Kiss*. She lives in Brooklyn, not far from where she grew up.

Kirk Citron ("Near Miss," pg. 24) is the founder of the digital advertising agency AKQA. He edits *The Long News*, and lives in San Francisco and New York City.

Craig A. Williams ("Mom's Favorite Movie of All Time," pg. 26) is the author of *Mom, Have You Seen My Leather Pants?* He writes from his home in Santa Monica, California.

Melissa Etheridge ("A Piece," pg. 29) has received fifteen Grammy Award nominations, winning two, as well as an Academy Award.

Jonathan Papernick ("Unexpected Pleasure," pg. 32) is the author of the short story collections *The Ascent of Eli Israel* and *There Is No Other.* He teaches fiction writing at Emerson College in Boston.

Michael Forster Rothbart ("Someday," pg. 35) is a photojournalist in upstate New York. He has two children.

Neal Pollack ("No Consolation," pg. 37) is the author of the memoirs *Stretch* and *Alternadad*, and the self-published novel *Jewball*, among other fine works. His freelance work has appeared in every English-language publication except the *New Yorker* and *Field & Stream*. He lives in Austin, Texas, with his wife and son.

Alaa Majeed ("Checkpoints," pg. 40) is an Iraqi journalist now living in Brooklyn. She has covered the news from both the Middle East and the United States for a variety of media outlets including the *Christian Science Monitor,* McClatchy, Pacifica Radio, *The New Yorker, The Nation,* and CBS, and she has conducted research for the nonprofit group, the Committee to Protect Journalists. She's currently coproducing documentaries for Al-Jazeera English and writing a book on Iraq.

Ruth Gruber ("The Assignment of My Life," pg. 43) became the youngest PhD in the world at the age of twenty before going on to become a journalist, photographer, writer, humanitarian, and Special Assistant to Secretary of the Interior Harold L. Ickes during World War II. She has written more than a dozen books, including *Haven,* which details her time as President Roosevelt–appointed escort for one thousand World War II refugees traveling from Naples to New York in 1944. A documentary, *Ahead of Time,* details Gruber's life from 1911–47, the period she writes about in her Moment.

Jeremy Toback ("Make Love, Not War," pg. 46) was a founding member, along with Pearl Jam's Stone Gossard, of seminal Seattle band, Brad. He is currently part of the beloved children's music duo, Renee & Jeremy, as well as the recently created alt-art rock group, Chop Love Carry Fire.

Matt Dojny ("Thank you, Lionel Richie," pg. 48) is a writer and artist who lives in Brooklyn. His debut novel will be published by Dzanc Books in April 2012.

Vivian Chum ("Assembly," pg. 49) is an attorney, writer, and executive director of a free football and SAT camp for at-risk youth.

Baratunde Thurston ("The Calling," pg. 52) is a Brooklyn-based standup comedian, political writer, and director of digital for the *Onion.* He resides in Brooklyn and is living his love.

Annie Leahy ("Missed Call," pg. 55) is the former executive producer for PopTech, a nonprofit social innovation company. A consultant for creative companies and nonprofits, she and her husband live in Portland, Maine.

Gregory Maguire ("Wicked Start," pg. 57) is the author of many books including *Wicked: The Life and Times of the Wicked Witch of the West*, which became the Broadway sensation, *Wicked*. He is the founder and codirector of Children's Literature New England, Incorporated, a nonprofit educational charity established in 1987.

Adam Theron-Lee Rensch ("Momento Mori," pg. 61) holds an MFA from Sarah Lawrence College and has received fellowships from the Yaddo Foundation. He divides his time between Ohio and New York, where he is at work on a memoir and a novel.

Elizabeth Gilbert ("The Secret Life of Parents," pg. 64) is the author of *Eat, Pray, Love*; *Committed*; *The Last American Man*; *Pilgrims*; and other works of nonfiction and fiction. Her Six-Word Memoir is "Me see world! Me write stories!"

Steve Almond ("John Updike Sent Me a Fan Letter (Once)," pg. 66) is the author of a bunch of books and at least two children. His latest story collection is *God Bless America*.

Mary Elizabeth Williams ("C-Listed," pg. 68) is a writer at Salon.com and author of the memoir *Gimme Shelter*.

Chris Sacca ("5RLG375," pg. 72) is a venture investor, private equity principal, entrepreneur, and public speaker who advises companies and nonprofits from Twitter to Livestrong, often from his home in Truckee, California. He was called "possibly the most influential businessman in America," by the *Wall Street Journal*.

Fiona Maazel ("My Blue Sticky," pg. 76) is the author of the novel *Last Last Chance* and has written for the *New York Times*, *Tin House*, *Bomb*, the *Mississippi Review*, the *Village Voice*, and Salon.com.

Tao Lin ("Lives," pg. 78) is the author of six books of fiction and poetry including *Richard Yates* and *Bed*. He lives in Brooklyn.

Bill Ayers ("Teachable Moment," pg. 81) is a longtime teacher/activist who lives and works in Chicago. **Ryan Alexander-Tanner** is a cartoonist and educator who lives in Portland, Oregon. See more of his work at www.ohyesverynice.com.

Nevenka Kurjakovic ("Disappointment," pg. 83) was born in the former Yugoslavia and educated in Europe and the United States. She has a graduate degree in linguistics from the University of Pittsburgh, speaks four languages, and reads and writes in two alphabets. She is currently working on a project called *Music Without Borders: The Relationship Between Music and Reconciliation in the Republics of Former Yugoslavia*.

Dan Goggin ("Divine Intervention," pg. 85) is the creator of the "Nunsense musical series." His shows have been presented in more than eight thousand productions and in twenty languages around the world.

Matthew Zapruder ("Poem for the Moment," pg. 87) is an editor for Wave Books and teaches as a member of the core faculty of UCR-Palm Desert's Low Residency MFA in Creative Writing. His most recent book is *Come On All You Ghosts*.

Dave Eggers ("Mr. Criche," pg. 90) is founder of the youth literary nonprofit 826 Valencia and the independent publisher, McSweeney's; and author of numerous books including *Zeitoun*, *What Is the What*, and *A Heartbreaking Work of Staggering Genius*.

Lori Sabian ("Cornrows," pg. 92) is a full-time parent and part-time educator for children and adults. Currently, she is working on embracing the unpredictability of both occupations.

Ellen O'Connell ("Dancing, in Green, to Ravel," pg. 94) has written for the *Nashville Review*, the *Louisville Review*, *Cerise Press*, *Redivider*, and *Ruminate*. She has just completed her first book and teaches literature at UC Santa Barbara.

Danny Davis ("Fluke," pg. 97) is one of the only riders to beat the world's most famous snowboarder, Shaun White, in the half pipe. Davis qualified for the 2010 Olympic half-pipe team in competition at the Mammoth Grand Prix in January 2010.

Micah Toub ("Persephone," pg. 100) is the author of *Growing Up Jung: Coming of Age as the Son of Two Shrinks*.

Rigoberto González ("Trash," pg. 101) is the author of eight books of poetry and prose. He is associate professor of English at Rutgers–Newark.

Cheryl Della Pietra ("Gonzo Girl," pg. 103) is a freelance copy editor and writer based in Connecticut. She has written for *Marie Claire*, *Redbook*, and *P.O.V. Magazine*, among others.

Josh Axelrad ("Rimshot," pg. 106) is a former professional blackjack player and author of the memoir *Repeat Until Rich*.

Piper Kerman ("Take the Wheel," pg. 109) is a vice president at Spitfire Strategies, a Washington, DC–based communications firm that works with foundations and nonprofits. She is the author of the memoir, *Orange Is the New Black: My Year Inside a Women's Prison*.

Haylee Harrell ("Black Like Me," pg. 111) is a freshman at the University of Utah.

Michael Castleman ("The Night My Mother Refused to Cook Dinner," pg. 113) is the author of twelve consumer health guides, among them *Building Bone Vitality* and *The New Healing Herbs*, and three mystery novels, most recently, *A Killing in Real Estate*.

Shalom Auslander ("Horns," pg. 115) is the author of *Beware of God: Stories*; *Foreskin's Lament*; and most recently, the novel *Hope: A Tragedy*.

Benjamin Percy ("What Would Roland Do?" pg. 117) is the author of the novel *The Wilding* and two books of stories, *Refresh, Refresh* and *The Language of Elk*. He is a regular contributor to *Esquire*.

Ashley Van Buren ("Fearless Flyer," pg. 120) is a writer and film production freelancer in New York City. She blogs at thebrow.org.

Dale Maharidge ("Hobo Beginnings," pg. 122) is an associate professor at the Graduate School of Journalism at Columbia University. **Michael S. Williamson**, who took the photo, is a staff photographer at the *Washington Post*.

Christoph Marshall ("Adopting My Son," pg. 124) is a biochemist and entrepreneur working with Avatar Biotechnologies to develop an AIDS vaccine.

Eddie Comacho ("Adopting My Dad," pg. 127) lives in Brooklyn.

Mira Ptacin ("Running," pg. 129) is a creative nonfiction and children's book author and founder and executive director of Freerange Nonfiction, a New York City reading series and storytelling collective.

L. Nichols ("At First Sight," pg. 132) is a Brooklyn-based artist/designer who posts new comics daily at www.dirtbetweenmytoes.com.

Julian Voloj ("Piazza San Marco," pg. 133) is a photographer living in Queens, New York.

Scott Muska ("First Kiss," pg. 134) is from Saxonburg, Pennsylvania, where he wrote his first words and had his first kiss. He currently works as a journalist and writer in Ocean City, Maryland.

Sara Lovelace ("The Crüe," pg 138) is a traveling writer, filmmaker, and yogi with an MFA in writing from the School of the Art Institute of Chicago. She makes her home on the sofas and air mattresses of her many friends across the country.

Alan Rabinowitz ("Uncaged ," pg. 140) is a zoologist, conservationist, and field biologist, and the president and CEO of Panthera, a nonprofit conservation organization devoted to protecting the world's thirty-six wildcat species. *Time* magazine has called him the "Indiana Jones of Wildlife Protection."

Ellen Sussman ("To the Rescue," pg. 143) is the author of the novels *French Lessons* and *On a Night Like This*. She is the editor of two anthologies, *Bad Girls: 26 Writers Misbehave* and *Dirty Words: A Literary Encyclopedia of Sex*.

Colin Nissan ("The Shed," pg. 145) writes TV commercials, humor essays for publications including *McSweeney's*, and books. Okay, one book. *Don't Be That Guy* came out last year.

Attila Kalamar ("Curtain Call," pg. 150) is a former air force sergeant who now works as a design engineer. He lives in Franklin, New Jersey, with his wife, Patti.

Kimberly Rose ("Photo Finish," pg. 153) has written for the *Fort Lauderdale Sun-Sentinel* and the *Miami Herald*. She enjoys writing flash fiction, six-word stories, and creative nonfiction about relationships and women's issues.

Laura Cathcart Robbins ("True Calm," pg. 155) is a full-time mother of two in Studio City, California.

Jeff Church ("Wally and Beaver," pg. 157) is a freelance creative director in advertising who lives in Hoboken, New Jersey, with his wife and son.

Caitlin Roper ("The Sign," pg. 160) is a magazine editor. She lives in San Francisco.

Sascha Rothchild ("The Thin Envelope," pg. 162) is a television and feature writer in Los Angeles and the author of *How To Get Divorced by 30*.

Elizabeth Jayne Liu ("Liner Notes," pg. 164) lives in Los Angeles with her daughter, husband, and website, www.flourishinprogress. com.

Aaron Huey ("If I Don't Die Today, I Will Marry Kristin Moore," pg. 166) is a contributing editor (photographer) for *Harper's Magazine* and a photojournalist who freelances regularly for *National Geographic*, *Harper's Magazine*, the *New Yorker*, *Smithsonian Magazine*, and the *New York Times*.

Wes Moore ("Boot Camp," pg. 170) is the author of *The Other Wes Moore: One Name and Two Fates—A Story of Tragedy and Hope*. He was a paratrooper and captain in the US Army, serving a combat tour of duty in Afghanistan with the 1st Brigade of the 82nd Airborne Division from 2005 to 2006.

Christine MacDonald ("Sunset Strip," pg. 171) is a writer and dancer based in her hometown of Waikiki, Hawaii. She is currently working on a memoir about her life as an exotic dancer.

Dan Baum ("Truth, Lies, and Audiotape," pg. 174) is the author of *Nine Lives: Death and Life in New Orleans*. He is currently working on a book about guns and the people who love them.

Saïd Sayrafiezadeh ("Stage Direction," pg. 176) is the author of the critically acclaimed memoir *When Skateboards Will Be Free*, and a 2010 recipient of the Whiting Writers' Award. His short stories and essays have appeared in the *New Yorker*, the *Paris Review*, *Granta*, and the *New York Times*.

Daniel DiClerico ("February 12, 2009, 9:14 a.m.," pg. 179) is a magazine editor who lives in Brooklyn with his wife and daughter.

James Cañón ("Balls Out," pg. 182) is the author of the international best seller *Tales from the Town of Widows*, adapted as the feature-length film *Without Men*.

Kristen Cosby ("Marooned," pg. 184) is a freelance writer and lecturer. Her work has appeared in the *Kenyon Review Online*, *Alaska Quarterly Review*, *Fourth Genre*, *Creative Nonfiction*, and *Pitt Med Magazine*. She is the recipient of the 2011 Normal School Prize in Nonfiction.

Steve Silberman ("Meeting Allen Ginsberg," pg. 187) is a science writer for *Wired* and other national magazines and lives with his husband, Keith Karraker, in San Francisco.

Alan Cheuse ("Those Old Keys," pg. 190) is National Public Radio's longtime "voice of books," and the author of four novels, three collections of short fiction, and the memoir *Fall Out of Heaven*. He teaches in the writing program at George Mason University and at the Squaw Valley Community of Writers.

Brian Evenson ("Mission Accomplished," pg. 191) is the author of ten books of fiction, including the novella *Baby Leg* and the novel *Last Days*, which won the American Library Association's award for Best Horror Novel of 2009.

Patrick Callahan ("Tell Me How This Ends," pg. 194) is the CFO of a real estate development company in Blue Bell, Pennsylvania, and the host of "This Week in Pro Football" on ESPN Radio in Philadelphia.

Jennifer Egan ("Keepsake," pg. 196) is a journalist and author of *The Invisible Circus, Emerald City and Other Stories, Look at Me,* and *The Keep.* Her most recent novel, *A Visit From the Goon Squad,* won both the 2011 Pulitzer Prize and National Book Critics Circle Award for Fiction.

Molly Lawless ("E-3: October 25, 1986," pg. 201) is a writer, illustrator, and native Bostonian currently living in Arlington, Virginia. She's working on her first book, *Hit By Pitch,* a work of graphic nonfiction about Ray Chapman. You can see more of her work at tyrnyx.wordpress.com.

Paul Miller aka DJ Spooky ("Landing," pg. 203) is a composer, multimedia artist, and writer. He's the author of two books on digital media, *Rhythm Science* and *Sound Unbound.*

Byron Case ("The Verdict," pg. 205) is a writer serving a life sentence at Crossroads Correctional Facility in Cameron, Missouri. His courtroom struggle is told in the book *The Skeptical Juror and the Trial of Byron Case* by John Allen. For more information, visit www.thepariahsyntax.blogspot.com.

Peter Kuper ("Nine Lives ," pg. 208) is the cofounder of *World War 3 Illustrated* and has appeared in publications around the world including *Mad* where he has done *Spy vs. Spy* every month since 1997.

Jessica Lutz ("My Front Line," pg. 210) is the author of two nonfiction books on Turkey and the city of Istanbul, the novel *Happy Hour* (written in Dutch), several short stories in English, and a children's book in German. Previously, she spent two decades reporting on issues of life and death on the eastern side of the Mediterranean for American and Dutch language media.

Julie Metz ("Instructions ," pg. 213) is a writer, graphic designer, artist, and author of *Perfection: A Memoir of Betrayal and Renewal.*

Julia Halprin Jackson ("2.10.01," pg. 215) has written fiction, nonfiction, and poetry that has appeared in anthologies by Scribes Valley Publishing, Flatmancrooked, and the American Diabetes Association, as well as the literary magazines *Fourteen Hills*, *Spectrum*, and *Catalyst*.

Deborah Copaken Kogan ("The Bloodless Coup," pg. 218) is the author of *Shutterbabe*, the bestselling memoir of her years as a war photographer, as well as *Between Here and April*, *Hell Is Other Parents*, and the forthcoming novel *The Red Book*.

Richard Ferguson ("Crying for Their Dog," pg. 222) is a Los Angeles–based writer, poet, and spoken-word performer who has been seen on *The Tonight Show*, at the Redcat Theater in Disney Hall, and at the New York City International Fringe Festival.

Ramona Pringle ("The Quest," pg. 224) is a multiplatform producer, digital journalist, actor, and member of the New Media Faculty at Ryerson University in Toronto.

Robin Wasserman ("Early Dismissal," pg. 229) is the author of several books for children and teens, including *Skinned*, *Hacking Harvard*, and the Seven Deadly Sins series.

Qraig R. de Groot ("Burning Up," pg. 232) lives in New York City with his boyfriend, Jamey Welch, in an apartment that lies approximately halfway between Madonna's first place of residence on East 4th Street and her current multiroomed show palace overlooking Central Park.

Judy Collins ("Maiden Days," pg. 236) is a Grammy Award–winning singer and songwriter who has been recording and performing for more than forty years.

Nadja Cada ("Just a Man," pg. 238) is a student at Ryerson University in Toronto.

Tamara Pokrupa-Nahanni ("Motherless," pg. 239) is a student at Ryerson University in Toronto.

Anthony Doerr ("The Ripple Effect," pg. 240) is the author of four books: *Memory Wall*, *The Shell Collector*, *About Grace*, and *Four Seasons in Rome*. He is currently a fellow of the John Simon Guggenheim Memorial Foundation.

Matthew Leader ("Positively 93rd Street," pg. 243) is a writer and lawyer in New York City.

Melissa Febos ("Smack Talk," pg. 245) is the author of the memoir *Whip Smart*. Her writing has been published in *Dissent*, *Bitch Magazine*, the *New York Times*, and *Hunger Mountain*. She is a 2010 and

2011 MacDowell Colony fellow and assistant professor of English at Utica College. She is at work on her first novel.

Arthur Suydam ("Firecracker," pg. 248) is an artist, author, and musician whose magazine work can be seen everywhere from *Heavy Metal* to *National Lampoon*. He has contributed to many comic books, including *Batman*, *Conan*, and *Tarzan*.

Andrew D. Scrimgeour ("The Silver Harmonica," pg. 250), dean of libraries at Drew University, has completed a book of Christmas stories. His essay, "A String of Bulbs Was Our Guiding Star" was published in the *New York Times*.

Kathy Ritchie ("Denial," pg. 253) is the founder of the blog, My Demented Mom.

Steve Anthony Leasure ("Mercy," pg. 255) lives in Douglasville, Georgia, where he is a quality manager for Dynamic Turbine.

Robert Joseph Levy ("The Hidden Dangers of Blood Magic," pg. 258) lives in Brooklyn, where his love spells have had more lasting success.

Emily Steinberg ("Blogging Toward Oblivion," pg. 260) is an artist and writer. Her graphic novel memoir *Graphic Therapy* is posted on *SMITH Magazine*. Her new illustrated stories series can be seen at http://emilycomics.blogspot.com.

Hope Rehak ("Tucked Away," pg. 263) is a poet, playwright, comedian, and essayist from Chicago. She attended Oberlin College on a scholarship from the Posse Foundation and graduated with a degree in English and creative writing. She is now living and working in Copenhagen, Denmark, and keeps a blog at hopegoesforth.blogspot.com

Jami Kempen ("Trusting Eyes," pg. 265) is a full-time student working toward her associate arts degree. She lives in Naples, Florida, with her daughter.

Jessica Anya Blau ("Ingress/Egress," pg. 266) is the author of the novels *Drinking Closer to Home* and *The Summer of Naked Swim Parties*. She lives in Baltimore and teaches at Goucher College.

Patrick Sauer ("Punchlines and Knockouts," pg. 270) is a freelance writer for publications including *Fast Company*, ESPN, *Huffington Post Humor*, *Whim Quarterly*, *Mr. Beller's Neighborhood*, and other low-paying outlets. More of his writing can be found at patricksauer.com.

Noah Scalin ("Head Case," pg. 274) is an artist, author, and designer based in Richmond, Virginia. He runs the socially conscious design and consulting firm Another Limited Rebellion and his art has been exhibited internationally in museums and galleries. His latest book, *365: A Daily Creativity Journal*, helps people start their own yearlong projects. His work can be viewed at www.NoahScalin.com.

Tony Schwartz ("In Pursuit of Optimism," pg. 274) is the founder of The Energy Project and author of *Be Excellent At Anything: The Four Keys to Transforming the Way We Work and Live*.

Katie Killacky ("Far Side," pg. 279) is a comedienne and actress from Chicago. She writes a blog based on life lessons from her mother, www.youreruiningmylife.blogspot.com.

Gillian Laub ("Family Jewels," pg. 282) is a New York–based photographer and author of *Testimony,* a book of portraits and journals from Israeli Jews, Israeli Arabs, and Palestinians and the second Intifada. Her photographs have appeared in the *New York Times Magazine, The New Yorker,* and *Time,* and she exhibits her work internationally.

Sara Barron ("Grandma's Dildo," pg. 284) is the author of *People Are Unappealing* and the forthcoming *Eating While Peeing (And Other Adventures).* She's appeared on Showtime's *This American Life,* NPR's *Weekend Edition,* NBC's *The Today Show,* and as a host at *The Moth*'s story-slams in New York City.

Ray Richmond ("Oprah Calling," pg. 287) is a journalist and author of four books, including the best seller *The Simpsons: A Complete Guide to Our Favorite Family.*

Karol Nielsen ("Vietnam, Revisited," pg. 290) is an adjunct professor in the department of writing and speech at New York University and author of the memoir *Black Elephants.*

Ashley Allen ("Conversation with My Dad," pg. 292) lives in Leesburg, Virginia—with her husband and three young sons—where she pursues her two passions: writing a book and becoming a rock star.

Ellen Jantzen ("Season's Greetings," pg. 295) is a photographer based in St. Louis.

Catherine Gilbert Murdock ("Revisionist History," pg. 297) is the author of the novels *Dairy Queen*, *Princess Ben*, and the forthcoming *Wisdom's Kiss*, as well as *Domesticating Drink*, a history of Prohibition.

Jennifer Thompson ("Forgiven," pg. 299) is the author, with Ronald Cotton, of *Picking Cotton: Our Memoir of Injustice and Redemption*. She speaks frequently about judicial reform. Watch a video of Thompson and Cotton in conversation at pickingcottonbook.com.

Jerry Ma ("Second Chance," pg. 302) is a graphic designer, illustrator, founder of Epic Proportions Art & Design, and art director of the groundbreaking Asian-American superhero comic anthology *Secret Identities*.

Mary Valle ("Moving On," pg. 304) is a contributing editor to the online magazine, Killing the Buddha. Her work has appeared in Salon.com, *Esquire*, and the *Los Angeles Times*.

Dar Wolnik ("Four Long Years," pg. 306) lives in New Orleans and works as a trainer and researcher within the farmers market movement. Her essay on the effect of the federal levee breaks on the local food system was included in the 2005 anthology *Do You Know What It Means to Miss New Orleans?* She writes on www.neworleanscanthrive .blogspot and www.frenchquarterbxb.com.

John B. Carnett ("Birth," pg. 307) is the staff photographer for *Popular Science* magazine.

Stephen Tobolowsky ("The Moth and the Window," pg. 309) is an actor who has been seen in many television shows including

Deadwood, *Heroes*, *Community*, and *Glee*. He may be best know for his role as Ned Ryerson in *Groundhog Day*.

Rebecca Woolf ("Tomorrowland," pg. 312) is the author of *Rockabye: From Wild to Child*, a memoir about how her life changed when she became a mom, based on her popular personal blog, *Girl's Gone Child*.

About the Editor / SMITH Magazine

©Kris Krüg/PopTech

SMITH Magazine founding editor **LARRY SMITH** coedited the *New York Times* bestseller *Not Quite What I Was Planning* and the Six-Word Memoir series, including *Six-Word Memoirs on Love & Heartbreak, I Can't Keep My Own Secrets,* and *It All Changed in an Instant.* He lives in New York City.

Books by SMITH Magazine

NOT QUITE WHAT I WAS PLANNING: SIX-WORD MEMOIRS®
by Writers Famous & Obscure

ISBN 978-0-06-137405-0 (paperback)

A *New York Times* bestseller and fascinating, addictively compelling illustrated collection of SIX-WORD MEMOIRS, alternately humorous, sad, and strange, from writers famous and obscure.

SIX-WORD MEMOIRS ON LOVE & HEARTBREAK
by Writers Famous & Obscure

ISBN 978-0-06-171462-7 (paperback)

Another collection of super-short stories—this time simple sagas exploring the complexities of the human heart.

IT ALL CHANGED IN AN INSTANT: MORE SIX-WORD MEMOIRS
by Writers Famous & Obscure

ISBN 978-0-06-171943-1 (paperback)

A thousand more glimpses of humanity— six words at a time.

I CAN'T KEEP MY OWN SECRETS: SIX-WORD MEMOIRS
by Teens Famous & Obscure

ISBN 978-0-06-172684-2 (paperback)

SIX-WORD MEMOIRS created by and for teens.